Critical Issues in Educational Leadership Series

Joseph Murphy, Series Editor

Distributed Leadership in Practice
JAMES P. SPILLANE AND JOHN B. DIAMOND, EDS.

Principal Accomplishments: How School Leaders Succeed
G. THOMAS BELLAMY, CONNIE L. FULMER, MICHAEL J. MURPHY, AND RODNEY MUTH

Balanced Leadership: How Effective Principals Manage Their Work
SHERYL BORIS-SCHACTER AND SONDRA LANGER

A New Agenda for Research in Educational Leadership
WILLIAM A. FIRESTONE AND CAROLYN RIEHL, EDS.

The Effective Principal: Instructional Leadership for High-Quality Learning
BARBARA SCOTT NELSON AND ANNETTE SASSI

Redesigning Accountability Systems for Education
SUSAN H. FUHRMAN AND RICHARD F. ELMORE, EDS.

Taking Account of Charter Schools: What's Happened and What's Next?
KATRINA E. BULKLEY AND PRISCILLA WOHLSTETTER, EDS.

Learning Together, Leading Together:
Changing Schools through Professional Learning Communities
SHIRLEY M. HORD, ED.

Who Governs Our Schools? Changing Roles and Responsibilities
DAVID T. CONLEY

School Districts and Instructional Renewal
AMY M. HIGHTOWER, MICHAEL S. KNAPP,
JULIE A. MARSH, AND MILBREY W. MCLAUGHLIN, EDS.

Effort and Excellence in Urban Classrooms:
Expecting—and Getting—Success with All Students
DICK CORBETT, BRUCE WILSON, AND BELINDA WILLIAMS

Developing Educational Leaders: A Working Model:
The Learning Community in Action
CYNTHIA J. NORRIS, BRUCE G. BARNETT, MARGARET R. BASOM, AND DIANE M. YERKES

Understanding and Assessing the Charter School Movement
JOSEPH MURPHY AND CATHERINE DUNN SHIFFMAN

School Choice in Urban America: Magnet Schools and the Pursuit of Equity
CLAIRE SMREKAR AND ELLEN GOLDRING

Lessons from High-Performing Hispanic Schools: Creating Learning Communities
PEDRO REYES, JAY D. SCRIBNER, AND ALICIA PAREDES SCRIBNER, EDS.

Schools for Sale: Why Free Market Policies
Won't Improve America's Schools, and What Will
ERNEST R. HOUSE

Reclaiming Educational Administration as a Caring Profession
LYNN G. BECK

Distributed Leadership in Practice

EDITED BY

James P. Spillane
John B. Diamond

Teachers College
Columbia University
New York and London

Published by Teachers College Press, 1234 Amsterdam Avenue,
New York, NY 10027

Library of Congress Cataloging-in-Publication Data

Distributed leadership in practice / edited by James P. Spillane,
John B. Diamond.
    p. cm.
  Includes bibliographical references and index.
  ISBN 978-0-8077-4806-0 (pbk. : alk. paper)—
  ISBN 978-0-8077-4807-7 (hardcover : alk. paper)
    1. Educational leadership—United States—Case studies.
  2. School management and organization—United States—Case
studies. I. Spillane, James P. II. Diamond, John B.
  LB2806.D57   2007
  371.2—dc22   2007009531

ISBN 978-0-8077-4806-0 (paper)
ISBN 978-0-8077-4807-7 (cloth)

Printed on acid-free paper
Manufactured in the United States of America

14 13 12 11 10 09 08 07   8 7 6 5 4 3 2 1

To the Memory of

Adam Roux

1979–2006

Contents

Acknowledgments

Books are collaborative endeavors; the pages that follow have benefited from the work of many hands and minds whose names do not make it onto the final pages. Special thanks go to the staff members of the schools we discuss in this volume who opened up their doors, allowing us to attend meetings, sit in classrooms, and generally hang out over many years. We are greatly indebted to these individuals, who go by pseudonym or are unnamed in the pages that follow, because if it was not for their generosity, openness, warmth, and frankness we never could have successfully undertaken this project.

The book would not have been possible if it was not for an outstanding interdisciplinary research team of postdoctoral fellows, graduate students, and undergraduate students at Northwestern University. Aside from the authors in this volume, we are especially grateful to Fred Brown, Loyiso Jita, Brenda Lin, Tondra Loder, and Antonia Randolph. Others who supported the completion of the manuscript include Wendy Angus and Kristy Cooper at Harvard, and Adee Braun and Brian Ellerbeck at Teachers College Press.

The book could not have been completed if it was not for the generous financial support for the Distributed Leadership Study from the Spencer Foundation and the National Science Foundation. Special thanks go to Jim Dietz and Elizabeth Vanderputten at the National Science Foundation for their ongoing support for the project. Northwestern University's School of Education and Social Policy, and Institute for Policy Research also provided extensive support for the project as well as a group of colleagues who contributed invaluable critique on the research. The Harvard Graduate School of Education also provided invaluable support and colleagueship. Spillane also gratefully acknowledges the support of the New Zealand Fulbright Committee, the Rockefeller Foundation, the Carnegie Corporation of New York, and the Institut National De Recherche Pedagogique in Lyon, France, which provided time and support for writing this manuscript. Diamond gratefully acknowledges the support of the National Academy of Education/Spencer Foundation Postdoctoral Fellowship Program, the William F. Milton Fund and the Radcliffe Institute for Advanced Study at Harvard University, and the Dean's Dissemination Fund at the Harvard Graduate School of Education.

Many individuals have contributed greatly to our thinking about distributed leadership over the past decade, far too many to mention by name here. Rather than commit the sin of omission, we mention none—you know who you are and we are very appreciative. We dedicate this volume to the memory of Adam Roux who as an undergraduate student in Learning and Organizational Change at Northwestern University's School of Education and Social Policy was our data manager for the project. Adam was a rare gem, a natural leader, a keen mind, who departed us far too early. We miss you, Adam! As always, our immediate and extended families have provided unwavering love and support for which we are greatly indebted.

Of course, none of these individuals or agencies are responsible for the pages that follow. We alone take that responsibility.

Distributed
Leadership
in Practice

Taking a Distributed Perspective

James P. Spillane
NORTHWESTERN UNIVERSITY

John B. Diamond
HARVARD UNIVERSITY

Distributed leadership has the attention of practitioners, professional developers, philanthropists, policymakers, and scholars. Some state and local governments have invested in promoting a distributed approach to leadership. Philanthropists have devoted millions to research and development work that favors, or at least acknowledges, a distributed approach. Professional developers, including some universities, have created programs for school practitioners that promote a distributed approach. Increasingly, scholars use a distributed perspective to frame their work (Firestone & Martinez, 2007; Leithwood, Mascall, Strauss, Sacks, Memon, & Yashkina, 2007; MacBeath & McGlynn, 2003; MacBeath, Oduro, & Waterhouse, 2004; Timperley, 2005).

The appeal of a distributed perspective lies partially in the ease with which it becomes many things to many people. Frequently used as a synonym for democratic leadership, shared leadership, collaborative leadership, and so on, the distributed perspective easily and effortlessly entered the discourse about school leadership and management. Usages vary. Some use it as though it were a blueprint or recipe for effective school leadership—yet another Holy Grail for improving schools. Others use it as a conceptual or analytical lens for investigating school leadership. Some move back and forth, sometimes unknowingly, between normative and theoretical stances. Such diversity in usage and understanding is to be expected; it is the way that ideas work in the world of practice, scholarship, and development. Ideas, as they percolate or trickle through various conversations, become understood in new ways, taking on new meanings and getting put to new uses. Some might say that ideas such as distributed leadership become diluted or muddled, but of course that conclusion assumes some pure original state. Perhaps the best we can hope for concerning distributed leadership—and any set of ideas, for that matter—is that they continue to be a part of conversations about school improvement.

Still, some commentators worry that distributed leadership's user-friendly qualities portend trouble. Some wonder whether distributed leadership is just a new label for old familiar constructs or ideas. The fear is that distributed leadership will become a catchall for any attempt to share leadership or delegate leadership to others (Harris, 2005). As a result, a distributed perspective could end up being everything and nothing at the same time. Does a distributed perspective offer a substantively different way of thinking about school leadership or is it simply another case of the emperor having no (new) clothes? Loose constructs pose problems for researchers and practitioners alike. For researchers, they contribute to fuzzy scholarship. For practitioners, while they ease exchanges, they often give a false sense of agreement and understanding among people as they talk past one another.

This book focuses on taking a distributed perspective to study school leadership and management. Our central question is this: What does it mean to take *a* distributed perspective? To address this question, we describe the core elements of a distributed perspective and investigate the entailments of taking this perspective to examine school leadership and management. Further, we consider the value added by adopting a distributed perspective in studies of school leadership and management. While our primary orientation in this book is as researchers, we do not see academics as having a monopoly on the collection and analysis of data. Instead, we believe that practitioners—school leaders, staff developers, and district policymakers— also can and should engage in research as part of their work. While practitioners' research orientations may differ in some respects from those of academics, the design efforts central to practice should be informed by diagnostic work, some of which can be carried out only by practitioners.

In this chapter, we outline what we mean by a distributed perspective on school leadership and management. Our aim is to articulate, as clearly and succinctly as possible, a distributed framework for investigating leadership and management in schools. Attempts at clarity often are misconstrued as pontificating. This is not our aim. Rather, we seek to explicate what we mean when we take a distributed perspective in the study of practice. We anticipate other interpretations and understandings and at times allude to these, not to disparage but rather to make our own meaning clear. We also should acknowledge that our own understandings continue to evolve as we continue with the theory-building work reported in this book.

LEADING AND MANAGING THE SCHOOLHOUSE

School leadership and management (often equated with school principals' work despite empirical evidence calling for more inclusive perspectives) are thought critical for successful schools. School-level factors matter when it comes to improving student learning and maintaining these improvements over time.

What Matters

Specifically, various lines of inquiry, from effective schools research to work on professional community, have identified key organizational functions that must be performed in order for schools to run effectively. A selective synthesis of the research suggests that these functions fall into three broad categories:

- Compass setting
- Human development
- Organizational development

Studies consistently have identified that both compass setting and maintaining a direction are critical for school success. This work puts emphasis on developing an instructional vision that is shared by members of the school staff (Bryk & Driscoll, 1985; Newmann & Wehlage, 1995). As one might expect, human capital development is also critical for a school to run effectively. This development happens through functions such as summative and formative monitoring of instruction and its improvement, support for individual and collective staff development and growth, and recognition of individual successes by school leaders. A third set of functions focuses on organizational development and includes developing and maintaining a school culture in which norms of trust, collaboration, and collective responsibility for student learning support ongoing conversations about instruction and its improvement.

Organizational development also involves procuring and distributing resources necessary for the work of school improvement, including materials, time, support, and compensation. This work frequently involves negotiating the environment beyond the schoolhouse walls. These three categories of organizational functions have been identified by numerous studies as essential elements for school improvement, and the school principal is often critical to ensuring that these organizational functions are addressed (Liberman, Falk, & Alexander, 1994; Rosenholtz, 1989a).

Some Definitional Issues

Many scholars distinguish *management* from *leadership* (Burns, 1978; Cuban, 1988). Management activity maintains, hopefully efficiently and effectively, current organizational arrangements and ways of doing school business; it centers on maintenance. Leadership activity, in contrast, involves influencing others to achieve new, hopefully desirable, ends; it frequently involves initiating changes designed to achieve existing or new goals. Typically, leadership activity involves transforming existing ways, upsetting business as usual in schools and classrooms, although the "managerial imperative" often dominates the work of school leaders (Cuban, 1988).

For the purpose of this book, we go with the popular definition of management: the maintenance of current organizational arrangements and ways of doing business. Our definition of leadership, however, departs somewhat from many popular definitions.

> *Leadership* refers to activities tied to the core work of the organization that are designed by organizational members to influence the motivation, knowledge, affect, or practices of other organizational members or that are understood by organizational members as intended to influence their motivation, knowledge, affect, or practices. (Spillane, 2006, pp. 11–12, emphasis in original)

Our definition excludes actions intended to influence relationships that are not tied to the school's core work. Of course, defining leadership in terms of the school's core work is not without its problems. We see the core work as teaching and learning, although some organizational theorists would point out correctly that for school staff, the core work might be preserving the school and their positions. Leadership is not always about change. As will be evident in Chapter 5, it also can be about resistance to change efforts.

Two aspects of this definition are important. First, our definition of leadership does not rest on evidence of effectiveness or a particular outcome being achieved. We define activities as leadership even if those who were intended to be influenced by an activity were not influenced. Second, in our definition, leadership needn't necessarily involve outcomes that are positive or beneficial. Leadership can influence people and organizations—indeed, entire societies—in directions that are not at all beneficial (Spillane, 2006).

Managerial activities, which are designed to produce stability, may differ substantially from leadership activities designed to promote change (Firestone, 1996). But what leaders do in the administrative and political realms, although often not directly and explicitly connected to changing some aspect of school life, may be an essential component of leadership in general, and leadership for instruction in particular. Indeed, efforts to change and efforts to preserve often are blended in the practice of leaders as tasks serving multiple agendas and functions. For example, maintaining scheduling arrangements for teachers that create opportunities for them to meet with one another can enable instructional innovation. Leaders who neglect managerial concerns, such as respecting the constraints on the daily schedule, may have difficulties leading change. Further, while the management versus leadership distinction is helpful as a theoretical tool, in practice it is often difficult to classify actions as purely managerial or purely leadership. The same activity can be designed to meet both maintenance and leadership goals.

THE PRACTICE OF LEADING AND MANAGING

A central argument in this book is that examining the day-to-day *practice* of leadership and management is an important line of inquiry and one that has been mostly neglected in both school administration and administrative studies in general. Much of the literature on leadership dwells on leaders and leadership structures, functions, and roles. Focusing mostly on *what* leaders do in broad and general terms, such accounts pay limited attention to the practice of leading and managing (Hallinger & Heck, 1996b). Knowing what leaders do is one thing, but a rich understanding of how, why, and when they do it, is essential if research is to contribute to improving the day-to-day practice of leading and managing schools. An in-depth analysis of the practice of leadership and management, not just the practice of leaders, merits the attention of scholars.

A practice or "action perspective sees the reality of management as a matter of actions" and encourages an approach to studying leadership and management that focuses on action rather than exclusively on structures, states, and designs (Eccles & Nohria, 1992, p. 13). Defining leadership and management as activity allows for the possibility that people in various positions in an organization might take on the work (Heifetz, 1994). It also foregrounds practice, an important move because "the strength of leadership as an influencing relation rests upon its effectiveness as activity" (Tucker, 1981, p. 25). In-depth analysis of leadership practice is rare but essential if we are to make progress in understanding school leadership (Heck & Hallinger, 1999).

Some scholars may find such claims overdrawn because of the sizable literature on leadership styles and approaches built up from analysis of collections of coherent practices. Although helpful, this work extracts leadership practice from its temporal context and in so doing ignores "the urgency of practice" (Bourdieu, 1981, p. 310). The confusion about attention to the practice of leadership and management results in part because the term is used in different ways. *Practice* is used to refer to the comprehensive enactment of the profession, a set of specific skills or behaviors, the counterpart of theory, and the actual doing of leadership in particular places and times.

A focus on practice highlights the immediacy of the interactions to which organizational actors must be sensitive and responsive. When a function like building and selling an instructional vision is reduced to a set of programmable strategies, abstracted out of the dynamic situations in which culture and practice actually operate, it becomes disconnected from the urgency of practice.

To study leadership activity, it is insufficient to generate thick descriptions based on observations of that practice. Because of this, we frame our efforts to understand practice in a particular way—from a distributed perspective. We do not equate practice simply with the actions of individual leaders. Indeed, while people's actions are certainly important in studying practice, we argue that in efforts to understand the practice of leading and managing schools, we must pay close attention to the interactions, not simply the actions. Many efforts to analyze practice never get beyond the actions of individuals or aggregating the actions of two or more individuals. Interactions are critical to the study of practice, and we need to observe from within a framework if we are to understand the internal dynamics of practice.

A DISTRIBUTED PERSPECTIVE

Frameworks for studying leadership practice are scarce and tend to privilege individual actions. Yet, any attempt to understand practice must identify explicitly the conceptual tools it brings to bear. If, for example, we see leadership practice—what leaders do and how they do it—as chiefly a function of individual knowledge and expertise, then that has implications for how we approach the collection and analysis of data. Most frameworks tend to focus chiefly on either individual agency or the role of macrostructure in shaping what leaders do, but downplay the day-to-day practice of leadership. Indeed, investigations of work practices in general require the development of new conceptual frameworks, "frameworks built out of concepts that speak directly to practice" (Pickering, 1992, p. 7).

A distributed perspective is a conceptual framework for thinking about and studying school leadership and management. As an analytical tool, it can be used to frame research on school leadership and management. It also can be thought of as a diagnostic tool for practitioners and interventionists. Like any analytical framework, it foregrounds some aspects of the phenomena under consideration and backgrounds others. A distributed perspective involves two aspects—the leader plus aspect and the practice aspect.

The Leader Plus Aspect

A distributed perspective acknowledges that the work of leading and managing schools involves multiple individuals. Moreover, leadership and management work involves more than what individuals in formal leadership positions do. People in formally designated leadership and management positions and those without any such designations can and do take responsibility for leading and managing the schoolhouse. In this way, leading and managing transcend formal positions (Frost, 2005; MacBeath, 2006). A distributed perspective then acknowledges and takes account of the work of all the individuals who have a hand in leadership and management practice. Pressing us to examine who performs what leadership and management functions or activities, a distributed perspective cautions against investigating school leadership and management by focusing chiefly on what formally designated leaders do.

The Practice Aspect

A distributed perspective foregrounds the *practice* of leading and managing, but there is more. A distributed perspective frames this practice in a particular way; it frames it as a product of the interactions of school *leaders*, *followers*, and aspects of their *situation*. This distributed view of leadership shifts focus from school principals and other formal and informal leaders to the web of leaders, followers, and their situations that gives form to leadership practice.

Investigating purposeful activity in its "natural habitat" is essential for the study of human cognition (Hutchins, 1995; Leont'ev, 1981; Pea, 1993). An individual's cognition cannot be understood merely as a function of mental capacity, because sense making is enabled (and constrained) by the situation in which it takes place (Resnick, 1991). The interdependence of the individual and the environment shows how human activity, as *distributed* in the interactive web of actors, artifacts, and the situation, is the appropriate unit of analysis for studying practice. Cognition is distributed through the environments' material and cultural artifacts and through other people in collaborative efforts to complete complex tasks (Latour, 1987; Pea, 1993).

From a distributed perspective, leadership practice takes shape in the interaction of leaders, followers, and their situation (Gronn, 2002; Spillane, Halverson, & Diamond, 2004). These three elements—leaders, followers, and situation—in interaction mutually constitute leadership practice.

Leaders. The term *school leader* often brings to mind the school principal who works as a lone ranger. But no one leader has the resources of time, energy, and expertise to lead alone. A distributed perspective moves beyond this image and presses us to attend to the constellation of leaders who exert (or attempt to exert) influences on school-based instructional practices. Our work has shown that leadership for instruction typically involves principals, assistant principals, teacher leaders, and classroom teachers who work independently as well as collaboratively to influence instruction. A critical challenge from a distributed leadership perspective is to unpack the ways in which multiple leaders' actions are interdependent (Gronn, 2003; Spillane, 2006; Spillane, Diamond, & Jita, 2000, 2003; Thompson, 1967).

From a distributed perspective, leadership is *stretched over* the work of multiple leaders. Using this perspective, we can begin to characterize the different types of co-leading. For instance, what we call *collaborated distribution* is carried out by multiple leaders working together at one time and place (e.g., leading a faculty meeting). In contrast, *collective distribution* highlights how the work of leaders performing separately can nonetheless be interdependent. For instance, two school leaders might divide the routine of teacher evaluation into formative and summative components. In doing this, they work on the same leadership task at different times, but their work is interdependent.

Finally, *coordinated distribution* refers to leadership routines that are performed in a sequence. For instance, leaders in the schools we studied all attempted to use data generated from standardized assessments to influence instruction. Using test data in this way required a sequence of steps that relied on the completion of previous steps. For example, test data often were repackaged to enhance their usefulness to leaders in discussions with faculty members during meetings. This repackaging of data involved a number of sequential steps, which included administering the assessments, reanalyzing the data, and determining their potential meaning for improving instruction.

Multiple leaders together have expertise and knowledge that exceed what individual leaders possess. This means that groups of leaders potentially have cognitive properties that are greater than the sum of their individual parts. Thus, leadership routines often are best examined as group or collective processes rather than as individual processes. While a major focus of the distributed perspective is the work of leaders, we also emphasize relations between leaders and followers.

Followers. Some take umbrage at the term *followers* because of its association with passivity. Others argue that distinguishing between followers and leaders is problematic because social influence is a two-way affair. We believe the distinction is important. People in schools move in and out of followership and leadership roles depending on the situation, and acknowledging and documenting these shifts is important. Further, not keeping the follower notion alive threatens to undermine attention to the role of followers in defining leadership practice. We define leadership as an influence relationship. Leaders influence followers by motivating actions, enhancing knowledge, and potentially shaping the practice of followers. These influences are connected to the core work of the organization—teaching and learning in classrooms—through teachers. Distinguishing between leaders and followers —at least analytically—helps build a deeper understanding of the nature of these influences and how leadership connects to classroom practice *through* followers.

However, these relationships, and the dynamics associated with them, are not unidirectional. Followers choose to listen to leaders and decide which leaders and leadership messages should be heeded and which should not (often without regard to leaders' official positions). As we have shown elsewhere, followers "construct" leaders as legitimate based on their perceptions of the leaders (Spillane, Hallett, & Diamond, 2003). Our ability to understand these dynamic, interactive relationships is enhanced by distinguishing between leaders and followers, and focusing on how followers make decisions about influences on themselves and their instructional practices. Further, in our scheme, followers are a defining element of leadership practice; in interaction with leaders and aspects of the situation, followers contribute to defining leadership practice.

Situation. Scholars have long recognized that the situation is a critical consideration in investigations of practice, including leadership and management practice. The situation of practice can make it more or less difficult to employ certain means and achieve certain ends. Contingency theory and work on situational leadership have established the importance of the situation to the work of leadership and management.

The circumstances of schools influence what leaders do as well as the effects of what they do on followers (Bossert, Dwyer, Rowan, & Lee, 1982; Hallinger & Murphy, 1987a; Murphy, 1991; Rosenholtz, 1989a). The complexity and uncertainty of the work performed by the organization, its size, and the complexity of its environment all influence its structural arrangements and performance (Galbraith, 1973; Scott, 1995). In education, the clarity and complexity of the instructional technology influence the extent to which school administrators coordinate and control the work of teachers. Similarly, the maturity of subordinates has been identified as an important variable in determining the most appropriate leadership model (Hersey & Blanchard, 1977). Whether a leader adopts a task-oriented or relation-oriented style depends on subordinates' job maturity (i.e., their capacity and ability to perform a task and their experience with a particular task) and psychological maturity (e.g., motivation, self-esteem, and confidence). Research in education suggests that schools with a more mature and stable staff are likely to have principals with more indirect leadership styles compared with schools with a younger and less stable staff (Dwyer, Lee, Rowan, & Bossert, 1983).

From a distributed perspective, however, aspects of the situation do not simply "affect" what school leaders do as some sort of independent variable(s); the situation is *constitutive* of leadership and management practice. As integral defining elements of practice, aspects of the situation such as organizational routines and tools in interaction with people define leadership and management practice. These aspects of the situation are not external to practice but are one of its core constituting elements. Hence, the practice of leading and managing is, to varying degrees, stretched over facets of the situation, including tools and routines. The situation is not something that is detached from practice or that influences practice from outside.

School leaders and teachers do not act directly on the world; instead their interactions are mediated by tools, routines, and other aspects of their situation (Wertsch, 1991). Tools, routines, and other aspects of the situation serve as go-betweens in interactions among people. Leadership and management practice takes shape in these interactions. In this way, aspects of the situation define practice in interaction with leaders and followers. These aspects of the situation, as realized in leadership practice, do not simply influence practice from the outside in by enabling people to execute their plans of action more or less efficiently. Instead, they give form to leadership practice in interaction with leaders and followers from the inside. Tools, routines, and other aspects of the situation bring some elements to the foreground in interactions while backgrounding other elements, and in this way they define what leaders and followers heed (Spillane, 2006).

Situation is both the medium for practice and an outcome of practice. As the medium for practice, aspects of the situation offer both affordances and constraints in leadership and management practice. In turn, leadership practice *also* can transform aspects of the situation over time as new routines or tools are designed and put in place. Hence, in our research, we attempt to explore both how aspects of the situation contribute to defining leadership and management practice and how leadership and management practice creates and re-creates aspects of the situation. From a distributed perspective, the challenge for researchers involves not only documenting those aspects of the situation that enable and constrain practice, but also capturing how these aspects of the situation are transformed in practice.

Shared or Collaborative?

Some who write under the umbrella of distributed leadership work on the assumption that the perspective privileges a shared or collaborative approach to leadership. School leaders, however, don't have to see eye-to-eye or even have to get along with one another to co-perform leadership routines and tasks. Leadership practice can be stretched over leaders, even when they are not striving for the same ends. When leaders don't see eye-to-eye, they still work as a collective in co-performing a leadership routine. Whether two or more leaders seek similar, different, or even opposing goals is just another dimension of the analysis.

A WORD ON METHODOLOGY

In the distributed leadership study from which this book originated, we used the distributed perspective outlined above to frame a theory-building study of the practice of leadership and management in urban elementary schools. This mixed-methods longitudinal study, funded by the National Science Foundation and the Spencer Foundation, was designed to make the "black box" of leadership practice more transparent through an in-depth analysis of school management and leadership. As one might expect in a theory-building study, the initial distributed framework evolved as we gathered and analyzed data. Further, we appropriated new conceptual tools to help us analyze and interrogate our data.

Our study involved 15 K–5 and K–8 schools located in the Chicago area. We selected eight schools as case study sites and seven schools as interview-only sites. We chose schools that were actively working to improve instruction but were at different stages in the reform process. Some schools had shown improvement in student achievement for less than 2 years, some for between 3 and 5 years, and others for between 5 and 10 years. Although we selected schools that were improving, the Chicago Public Schools placed two of them on academic probation during our study. Selecting schools at different stages of the reform process provided important theoretical leverage for our examination of leadership practice.

We also chose schools with distinct demographic characteristics in their student populations. Among our case study sites, for example, four schools were predominantly African American, two were predominantly Mexican American, and two were at least 40% White and contained moderate-sized Asian and Latino populations. Table 1.1 shows the schools' demographic characteristics.

We spent 50–70 days per academic year in the case study sites between 1999 and 2003. In these sites, data collection included semistructured interviews with school leaders, interviews with classroom teachers, observation and shadowing of school leaders, classroom observations, document reviews, teacher and principal questionnaires, a social network survey, and videos of school leadership activities.

Because this was a multisite cross-case analysis, we developed interview and observation protocols to be used in each site and met regularly as a research team to ensure that the data were collected in a consistent manner across sites. We pursued several lines of analysis based on the distributed leadership framework and used our team meeting as a location for discussing and modifying these analytical activities. This was a particularly useful process for helping us identify and follow up on crosscutting themes that emerged in our data collection and analysis. We were assisted in data analysis by the computer program Nu*Dist 4.0 and its subsequent iterations (N6 in particular).

Table 1.1. Demographics for Schools in Study

School	Student Enrollment	Low Income (%)	Black (%)	White (%)	Hispanic (%)	Asian (%)
SCHOOL A	750–1,000	90–100	100	0	0	0
SCHOOL B	1,000–1,500	60–70	<10	40–50	20–30	20–30
SCHOOL C	1,000–1,500	70–80	<10	40–50	10–20	30–40
SCHOOL D	250–500	90–100	100	0	0	0
SCHOOL E	750–1,000	90–100	<10	0	90–100	0
SCHOOL F	250–500	90–100	100	0	0	0
SCHOOL G	1,000–1,500	90–100	100	0	0	0
SCHOOL H	1,000–1,500	90–100	<10	<10	80–90	<10

BOOK OVERVIEW

Each chapter focuses on the case of a different school (with exception of Chapters 3 and 6, which highlight different elements of the same school) and foregrounds different leadership functions, what we might term macro-functions, such as professional development or building a collaborative organizational culture. While some chapters foreground leadership functions that have to do with human development, others foreground organizational functions tied to organizational development. A distributed perspective frames all chapters; hence, the practice of leading and managing is central and understood as taking shape in the interactions of leaders, followers, and aspects of the situation. Further, relations between the practice of leadership and classroom practice are central in all the cases. This represents a departure from some work on school leadership where relations between leadership and instruction rarely are made explicit. Indeed, Chapters 6 and 7 in particular show how one key aspect of instruction—the school subject—is a potentially powerful explanatory variable in leadership practice.

Chapter 2 focuses on a key leadership function—monitoring instruction—through a case study of Hillside School. The Hillside case examines how, despite heavy administrative demands, the school's leadership team forged links between leadership practice and teaching practice by designing and implementing a number of organizational routines. Leaders at Hillside used aspects of the situation—tools of various sorts—to connect leadership practice and teaching practice. At Hillside, two types of tools—boundary practices and boundary objects—contributed to the establishment of direct links between key instructional leadership practice and classroom instruction. Amy Coldren describes how boundary practices and boundary objects worked at Hillside to connect leadership practice and instructional practice. This chapter unpacks how aspects of the situation define leadership practice by framing the interactions among leaders and followers.

Chapter 3 also focuses on aspects of the situation, examining how leadership practice at Adams School involved reshaping key aspects of the situation —routines and tools—in order to build professional community among teachers and to develop teachers' knowledge and skill. The chapter unpacks relations between the practice of leadership and two key leadership functions —professional development and creating a collaborative organizational culture. The chapter examines how leadership practice shapes some of the key organizational routines and tools and, in turn, how these routines and tools shape leadership practice. This analysis views the school community as a *system of practice*—a network of routines that enable (and indeed constrain) complex webs of practice in organizations. Systems of practice are composed of people and tools such as policies, programs, and procedures. School leaders at Adams built the Breakfast Club routine, a monthly gathering for teachers to discuss research articles relevant to their teaching, to enable teachers to share professional knowledge and build a professional community centered on teaching and its improvement. Richard Halverson goes on to examine how other leadership routines—for example, the Five-Week Assessment routine—evolved out of the Breakfast Club routine.

Chapter 4 explores the practice of leadership related to two other leadership functions—raising teacher expectations for students and holding teachers accountable for student learning—through the case of Kelly School. The Kelly case explores the practice of leadership designed to raise teachers' expectations for low-income, African American students and increase teachers' sense of responsibility for student learning. John Diamond maps the leadership routines associated with efforts to raise teachers' expectations and develop teachers' sense of responsibility for student achievement. Specifically, he examines how particular routines connect with leadership functions thought critical to school improvement. Further, he examines the performance of these routines—exploring how the practice of leadership is stretched over leaders and aspects of the situation.

Chapter 5 illustrates the challenges involved in leading change, especially when a new leadership inherits an existing staff and is intent on changing business as usual. The Costen case examines a new principal's struggle for credibility with staff when she takes over a school. Relying on her positional authority, Mrs. Kox disrupts the established order at Costen as she attempts to implement new organizational routines in an effort to improve teaching and learning. Mrs. Kox's use of her authority to establish new routines designed to deprivatize and systematically monitor classroom instruction undermines her credibility in the eyes of many teachers at Costen, some of whom openly challenge her leadership efforts. Tim Hallett uses this case to illuminate how leadership practice takes shape in the interactions between leaders and followers as mediated by aspects of the situation.

In Chapter 6, Jennifer Sherer explores leadership practice at Adams School, complementing Halverson's case by taking an in-depth look at how language arts becomes prioritized over mathematics in leadership practice. In this case, Sherer adopts a comparative approach contrasting leadership practice for mathematics with leadership practice for language arts at Adams. The case documents how school leaders' intentions and plans are not always reflected in their actual practice. While school leaders view both mathematics and language arts as high priorities, and while they create similar leadership routines in these two subjects, in the actual performance of these routines language arts becomes prioritized over mathematics. Sherer unpacks how this prioritization comes to pass in leadership practice.

In Chapter 7, Patricia Burch explores leadership practice at Baxter School, a school with a strong commitment to involving teachers in school-level decisionmaking and an elaborate infrastructure designed to enable this participation. This chapter supports and extends Sherer's chapter by exploring how school subjects play a critical role in leadership practice. Specifically, Burch explores the relationship between subject matter and the ways in which teachers participated in leading instructional improvement, showing that the leadership communities that developed around efforts to improve instruction at Baxter differed substantially for literacy as compared with mathematics. Teachers involved in literacy reforms sought myriad ways to participate in leading reform of literacy instruction, with the school's literacy coordinators and principal welcoming and nurturing this initiative. In contrast, in mathematics, one teacher primarily set the agenda for instructional reform, while other teachers largely followed that agenda and did not seek out leadership opportunities to the same degree as teachers in the literacy community. These dynamics illuminate how the school subject is a critical consideration when it comes to leadership practice, even in elementary schools where subject-matter departments and specializations are rare.

Chapter 8 explores the crosscutting themes from the various cases focusing on three issues. First, we use examples from the cases to consider the entailments of taking a distributed perspective on leadership and management. While recognizing that others may have definitions that deviate from ours, we present our perspective, as a group of researchers, on what it means to take a distributed perspective on leadership and management. Second, we highlight what the cases tell us about the utility or value of taking a distributed perspective. We illustrate how using this perspective can lead to new insights about leading and managing schools. Third, we discuss some of the theoretical, empirical, and practical challenges associated with taking a distributed perspective.

2

Spanning the Boundary Between School Leadership and Classroom Instruction at Hillside Elementary School

Amy F. Coldren
NORTHWESTERN UNIVERSITY

Barbara Nelson,[1] the long-time principal of Hillside Elementary School in Chicago, maintained a commanding presence—when she talked, people sat up and listened. Her style at work was all business—direct and no-nonsense—but she commanded respect from those around her.

Mrs. Nelson, as her staff referred to her, ran a tight ship and was tirelessly dedicated to the children and families she worked to serve every day. In fact, she knew virtually each of Hillside's more than 1,000 students by name. On the playground one morning before school, she slowly meandered in and out of rows of students who were lined up to go to their classrooms, stopping periodically to talk to them about current, pressing issues. She asked one boy if he had completed his science project that was past due and warned, "Because if you don't, Oscar, you will be spending every day after school with me!" When she came to a seventh grader who looked at her shyly, Mrs. Nelson asked with genuine interest, "Katie, how did your speech go?" The girl replied, "I was really nervous!" Mrs. Nelson not only addressed students by name; she knew what was happening in their lives.

Although dedicated to the lives and education of her students, Mrs. Nelson described her professional role largely in terms of the administrative work that was required to run such a large school, rather than in terms of providing leadership for instruction. She explained:

> I think my major job is just to make sure that everything works for the kids. And looking for resources, trying to make sure that things are there that we need, trying to make sure the teachers have as much time as possible to actually do their job, keeping the budgets balanced, making sure everybody gets paid, making sure the building is cleaned, make sure the buses are running. A lot of administrivia, which is very different from when I first became a principal.

In this respect, Mrs. Nelson is the norm rather than the exception among U.S. school principals. Most teachers report that their principals spend little time talking with them about instructional matters (Goldring & Cohen-Vogel, 1999).

However, despite heavy administrative demands, Mrs. Nelson was able to orchestrate ways to influence classroom instruction, working to connect her work as a leader and manager to that of the teachers. Through the use of organizational routines and tools, Mrs. Nelson established direct links between key leadership activities and classroom teaching and learning that enabled her to influence classroom instruction. I refer to these routines and tools as boundary practices and boundary objects. A *boundary practice* is an organizational routine that sustains connections between communities of practice or different constituencies and provides an ongoing forum for mutual engagement (Wenger, 1998). A *boundary object* is a tool or artifact that inhabits several intersecting social worlds and serves to coordinate the perspectives of various constituencies for some purpose (Star, 1989; Star & Griesemer, 1989; Wenger, 1998).

In this chapter, I explore how organizational routines and tools at Hillside served as boundary objects and boundary practices, enabling Mrs. Nelson to establish and maintain connections between school leadership activities and classroom teaching and learning. From a distributed leadership perspective, routines and tools, as aspects of the situation, are a key constituting component of leadership practice; this chapter examines how routines and tools frame interactions between leaders and followers and thereby define and are defined by leadership practice.

Leadership, and leadership for instruction in particular, plays a pivotal role in effective schools (Krug, 1992). Although instructional leadership often is equated with administrators observing teachers and conducting evaluations, it can involve a variety of activities, including defining a school mission, managing curriculum and instruction, supervising teaching, monitoring student progress, and promoting a positive instructional climate (Krug, 1992). In this chapter, I illustrate how one principal designed and appropriated organizational routines and tools to engage in leadership activities that go beyond the typified teacher observation and evaluation process. Cultivating a better understanding of the pivotal role of organizational routines and tools in school leadership will contribute to our knowledge of how leadership practice is distributed across a situation.

SETTING THE STAGE

The descendent of German and Scotch grandparents who originally settled not far from where Hillside is now located, Mrs. Nelson served the Chicago Public Schools for almost 40 years. For more than a decade she taught first grade and reading before taking her first administrative position as an assistant principal and counselor. Several additional administrative positions followed until she was selected as principal of Hillside, where she remained for more than 15 years.

Hillside, a massive three-story building with a stately, yellow brick façade, once housed a high school. Today, it is a K–8 "choice" school that serves over 1,000 students and has over 50 teachers. At least 93% of its students are Latino (many of whom speak English as a second language), and 95% come from low-income families.

Although Hillside readily falls into the category of "poor inner-city school," it has defied the usual fate of such schools. Throughout Mrs. Nelson's tenure, student test scores rose steadily, and the teaching staff remained stable. Teachers were invested in widespread and sustained professional development that challenged their teaching. Although Mrs. Nelson's commanding presence and devotion contributed to the school's increasing success, her leadership style and commitment alone could not account for the change. Her role as a schoolwide instructional leader and, in particular, the direct links she forged between school leadership activities and classroom teaching are critical for understanding improvement efforts at Hillside.

Leadership at Hillside was distributed across various administrators, counselors, teachers, and parents. Still, Mrs. Nelson emerged as one of the primary leaders of classroom instruction. I examine leadership practice at Hillside from her perspective in order to explore the role of organizational routines and tools in making and maintaining connections between leadership practice and teaching practice. Through the careful use of organizational routines and tools, she was able to monitor and improve the quality of classroom teaching and learning throughout the school.

DATA AND ANALYSIS

We collected data at Hillside between February 1999 and June 2000. For this chapter, I relied primarily on 40 interviews with teachers and leaders (including multiple interviews with several individuals) and detailed field notes of 18 grade-level meetings and 5 faculty meetings.

To conduct the analysis, I developed a coding scheme that included nodes for boundary practices, boundary objects, and dimension of instruction. I coded any instance of an organizational routine that connected the school principal and teachers (e.g., a regular meeting) as a boundary practice. I coded any tool that was used to coordinate teachers' and administrators' perspectives or actions (e.g., test scores) as a boundary object. Finally, by dimension of instruction I mean the aspect of instruction the boundary practice or object addressed, including general pedagogy, pedagogical content, assessment, curriculum/materials, and students. Coding the data according to this scheme allowed me to identify instances in which school personnel used boundary practices and objects and to examine the purposes for which they were used. Finally, to gauge the principal's influence on classroom teaching, I examined excerpts from interviews and meetings in which teachers cited the principal when discussing their work.

MAKING CONNECTIONS TO TEACHING AND LEARNING

School principals assume three important roles in their work—managerial, instructional, and political[2] (Cuban, 1988). The managerial role encompasses work necessary to maintain organizational stability in the school, including tasks such as planning, gathering and dispersing information, budgeting, hiring, scheduling, and maintaining the building. The instructional role encompasses work that relates to the instructional unit—the intersection of teachers, students, and materials (Cohen & Ball, 1998). Examples of principal activities that fall within the instructional role include defining a school's instructional mission, managing the instructional program through formal and informal teacher supervision and evaluation, and promoting professional growth (Cuban, 1988; Hallinger & Murphy, 1987a, 1987b; Krug, 1992).

School principals historically have engaged more in managerial activities than in instructional ones, a tendency Cuban (1988) refers to as the "managerial imperative." At Hillside, Mrs. Nelson reported that the managerial imperative was strong and had become even stronger during her tenure in the principal's office. She explained that a shift from centralized district governance to site-based management several years earlier increased her administrative duties and took time away from instructional matters.

So therefore, you're not probably as involved in the instructional program as I was in the past. Although I do monitor and visit classrooms and all those things, I would prefer to do a lot more of it and really get more strongly involved in that. But because of the amount of other things that we have to do nowadays, it kind of cuts back on that.

Despite her desire to spend more time in the instructional role, Mrs. Nelson found her time at Hillside increasingly dominated by administrative duties.

Not surprisingly, the administrative structure of schools is often only "loosely coupled" to classroom teaching and learning (Meyer & Rowan, 1978). While first impressions might suggest that Hillside fits this general pattern, a closer examination of Mrs. Nelson's work suggests otherwise. Leadership and management practice at Hillside illuminates how school administrators, using organizational routines and tools, can influence classroom instruction schoolwide. Although Mrs. Nelson herself carried out much of the managerial work that was necessary to keep her school running smoothly, she also devoted time and energy to her instructional role by using boundary practices and boundary objects to establish and maintain connections with classroom teaching practices. As a key part of the situation, these routines and tools helped to define, and also were defined in and through, leadership practice.

ORGANIZATIONAL ROUTINES AND TOOLS AS BOUNDARY PRACTICES AND BOUNDARY OBJECTS

Mrs. Nelson used organizational routines and tools, specifically boundary practices and boundary objects, to establish and maintain schoolwide connections to teaching and learning. Boundary practices and boundary objects go hand in hand, and the former often involve the use of the latter. In order to maintain regular connections to teaching practice, Mrs. Nelson established a variety of boundary practices using boundary objects that included writing folders, student assessments, and lesson plans. Below, I examine these boundary practices along with the boundary objects that accompanied them, paying particular attention to how they defined and were defined by leadership practice at Hillside.

Writing Folder Review Routine

For Mrs. Nelson, the ability to write and communicate clearly was a key factor in the success of minority children. She explained:

It's part of my whole drive about perceptions that people have of minority children. And, you know, being able to speak and being able to write are two very important components of people perceiving you as being an educated person. . . . When I started reading children's writing, it didn't make any sense. There was no beginning. There was no middle. There was no end. The spelling was atrocious. Everything, you know, it looked—it didn't look like we cared, and that bothered me. Because as I said, I want our children to be able to have options and to be able to get in a good high school, and . . . when they write things, even a composition about a particular title, you can find out so much about kids and what they think and how they feel.

Acting on these beliefs, Mrs. Nelson worked to establish a stronger connection between her efforts to improve teaching and learning at Hillside and classroom writing instruction, requiring teachers to regularly submit students' writing to her. On a monthly basis from October through April, every teacher submitted a folder that contained one composition written by each student in the class. Establishing a new organizational routine at Hillside designed to influence writing instruction, Mrs. Nelson regularly read each student's work and provided the teachers and students with written feedback. This routine was a boundary practice in that it sustained a regular connection between Mrs. Nelson and both teachers and students, providing an ongoing forum for their mutual engagement in seeking to improve student writing and writing instruction.

Using the writing folder review routine as a lever to influence writing instruction across classrooms, Mrs. Nelson explained:

You know, I can tell a lot of what's happening in the classroom by just reading folders and providing feedback to teachers. I can see people who maybe need to work a little on certain things. . . . So I thought it was a good way for me to get kind of a snapshot of what's happening and what people are doing in this school. It forced teachers to actually teach writing as a subject and not just as a homework assignment and encouraged them to use the writing as an integrated thing, not as a stand-alone.

The writing folder routine provided Mrs. Nelson with a window into the world of the classroom, enabling her to monitor instruction—a key leadership function. At the same time, this practice defined writing instruction as a priority by requiring teachers to regularly teach writing "as a subject."

In addition, the writing folder review routine connected Mrs. Nelson to teachers *and* students, two key components of the instructional unit (Cohen & Ball, 1998). By monitoring the quality of students' writing along with their understanding of the writing process and by giving them written feedback, Mrs. Nelson worked to improve student learning, encouraging students to work harder and giving them pointers on how to improve their writing. For example, Ms. Crawford, a fifth-grade teacher, submitted her students' expository compositions on "How to Eat an Oreo Cookie." She showed me the compositions complete with Mrs. Nelson's written comments, ranging from those of her top students to those of students who were struggling. All of the submissions included multiple drafts of each composition so that Mrs. Nelson could see the progression of each student's work, as well as a cover page that included the student's name, the composition's title, and how the teacher scored it along five dimensions—focus, support, organization, conventions, and integration. On the cover page of one student's paper, Mrs. Nelson had written, "Needs work on support and spelling corrections," and signed her initials. She also had made a comment in the text of a previous draft of the work that said, "Nice beginning." On another student's paper she wrote more extensively, "Needs *more* details. Paragraphs should be 3–4 sentences. Watch your sentences. Start with a capital letter & end with a period." On that paper she also had written a comment to Ms. Crawford, circling the student's score for "support" and writing, "Not enough support," implying that Ms. Crawford had scored it too high. Mrs. Nelson wrote on another, "Better, but still needs work. Not a 30" [referring to the total score]. Hence, Mrs. Nelson's notes allowed her to interact with students directly about their writing in order to improve it.

The writing folder review routine simultaneously allowed Mrs. Nelson to connect with the teachers. She explained:

> Well, I write notes to every single classroom every single month. And some of it, you know, I try to have it be constructive criticism. I try to give specific things that maybe the class might want to work on, and hopefully the teacher will say, "Well if the class needs to work on it, that probably means I need to work on it." And certainly, you know, when people come in for their final evaluations or if I've written a note—because I keep copies of the notes. I have them on file. When I do evaluations . . . if I'm continually writing to a teacher, you know, "Please work with your children on making sure that their paragraphs are longer than one sentence," and then at the end of the year they're still writing one-sentence paragraphs, I think this is a person who doesn't get the message or is not really interested in improving themselves or their children. So it figures into the final

evaluation—into the summative evaluation. But . . . if someone's having a real difficulty, I have no problem with talking to them personally about it.

The writing folder review routine held teachers accountable for teaching writing and enabled Mrs. Nelson to expand the teachers' professional capacity to teach it.

To improve writing instruction and student writing, Mrs. Nelson used the writing folder review routine to connect with two of the three constitutive elements of the instructional unit: teachers and students. She targeted teachers by holding them accountable through teacher evaluations and by engaging in personal conversations with them, if necessary, about areas needing improvement. She targeted students by monitoring their work and providing them with written feedback, teaching them what constitutes good writing. In essence, she used this routine as a way to teach both students and teachers about writing. Moreover, by simultaneously addressing teachers and students, she was more likely to effect change than if she had targeted only one or the other.

Teachers at Hillside reported that the writing folder review routine had an impact on their writing instruction. For example, referring to her students' work on a writing project, Ms. Crawford described how this routine changed her approach to writing instruction:

> I switch my whole day around so they get—they get almost an hour to work on this because I realize all these different issues and problems that the kids have because I can't write the stories for them. I have received notes from Mrs. Nelson. We have to turn in compositions monthly. . . . But that is what I've had to change in my approach this year is giving them more time to think, more time to work, more time to review the process. You know, review the criteria. You have to have this, this, and this. You have to have detailed sentences. . . . More time. That's what I've had to do.

For Ms. Crawford, submitting writing folders to Mrs. Nelson and receiving feedback prompted her to increase the amount of time she devoted to writing instruction. In addition, recognizing Mrs. Nelson's emphasis on the subject, she made a point to "review the criteria" for good writing with her students.

The Curriculum Coordinator, who in addition to her administrative duties taught an accelerated language arts class, described her own experience with the writing folders.

A piece from every student, but you might select the best pieces they produce. You put them in and then Mrs. Nelson reads them, and she hands you back a note commenting on them, where she thinks there's strengths, where she thinks there's weaknesses, and you share that with the students and, of course, you heed it yourself and try to do whatever she's advised. And I was very impressed when I was getting those writing folders back. I was impressed. You know she would comment on your vocabulary, which I worked very hard on. It was a big thing with me to beef up the vocabulary. She did take note of that. She did take note of how good they were editing their work because she wants to see the edited and the unedited version of the writing. You have to staple that together, which to me is fantastic because you don't know what the teacher has done until you see the rough and the finished. I've never heard of another principal doing this. To me, it's phenomenal that this woman makes time in her life to do this, to read these. And everyone talks about it. Everyone talks about it . . . the staff, the teachers. The teachers all talk about it. They're intimidated by it to a certain extent, but they've learned from it, they've grown from it, and when you look at our . . . writing scores compared to other schools [that are] comparable [in the] socioeconomic and ethnic area, it's incredible. I mean our scores are so much higher, and that's the reason they're higher.

These teachers' accounts illustrate how the writing folder review routine forged a tight connection between Mrs. Nelson's practice as an administrator and teachers' classroom practice.

The writing folder review routine sustained a regular connection about writing instruction between Mrs. Nelson and the teachers throughout the school year. The writing folders were an *ongoing* forum for mutual engagement (Wenger, 1998); this practice was routine at Hillside, a known procedure that both constituencies executed regularly (Zollo & Winter, 1998). Organizational routines provide an efficient means of accomplishing organizational functions such as monitoring classroom instruction. When a practice becomes routine, participants do not have to negotiate and renegotiate what is expected of them each time they engage in it. Rather, they come to know what the practice requires of them and what they can expect from it in return. Mrs. Nelson routinized the practice of reviewing writing folders, regularly providing leadership for writing instruction in every classroom, for almost 1,000 students and their teachers. Without the efficiency of this organizational routine, it is doubtful that Mrs. Nelson would have been able to exert such ongoing and widespread influence on instruction.

In the writing folder review routine, the folders and their contents (i.e., the students' writing samples and teachers' scoring rubrics), together with Mrs. Nelson's written feedback, were boundary objects around which she and the teachers interacted. The tools embedded in the writing folder review routine—student writing samples and teachers' scoring of these samples—focused the interactions between Mrs. Nelson and the teachers around the writing lessons as well as around students' work and writing achievement. In this way, these tools helped to define leadership and management practice.

In the literature on boundary objects, this construct has been used to analyze instances in which the constituencies employing the boundary object do not maintain vastly different power or status. Therefore, the constituencies operate on more or less an even playing field when it comes to the design, use, negotiation, and renegotiation of boundary objects whose purpose is to coordinate their perspectives or actions. When applying this construct to the study of school leadership, however, leaders such as principals are likely to have more power than teachers and students due in part to their formally designated leadership position in the school. Thus, when examining the use of boundary objects in instructional leadership, one cannot assume that a boundary object is used to "coordinate" the perspectives of a principal and teachers, implying that they occupy an even playing field and might meet in the middle. Rather, in this case, Mrs. Nelson designed the writing folder review routine for the purpose of bringing the teachers' thinking and practice in line with her own expectations for writing and writing instruction. In other words, she used this organizational routine to shape the teachers' thinking and practice (and students' thinking and practice) in a way that was consistent with her views and goals for student writing. This shaping is what instructional leaders do—they define a schoolwide mission and help others to achieve it (Cuban, 1988). As part of her role as instructional leader, Mrs. Nelson defined a schoolwide mission related to writing and established an organizational routine to achieve that mission. The writing folder review routine was the mechanism that allowed Mrs. Nelson to accomplish her mission of fostering students who can write and communicate clearly and present themselves in the world as educated. Mrs. Nelson's leadership practice was "stretched over" the situation, particularly this organizational routine and its embedded tools. This boundary practice, together with its boundary objects, led to a tighter coupling between the administration and classroom practice at Hillside.

Student Assessment Data as a Leadership Tool

Chicago Public School policy holds schools accountable for student achievement as measured by standardized test scores. As one might expect, standardized tests feature prominently in many schools, including Hillside.[3] Mrs. Nelson believed that one of her roles as principal was to analyze test scores to help teachers plan and improve the instructional program. She said:

> I think my major role is to be a facilitator, but certainly also to look at children's progress over time. To look at test results, to analyze— help teachers analyze results. Where are our strengths? Where are our weaknesses? What do we need to work on? You know, when we get standardized test results back, you know, looking at item analysis and so on and saying, "Well we did real well in this section, we didn't [do] so well in this section. What do we need to do to make sure that we're going to be—the kids are going to be more successful?" . . . So trying to help people focus on areas of deficit and, you know, kind of cheering for the items that we do well on.

Mrs. Nelson viewed assessments of all kinds, and not just standardized tests, as an important tool for instruction.

> I try to use any assessment as really a way to plan the instructional program. I don't look at it necessarily as a final result. If children are doing poorly, I think we need to look at ourselves and not at the kids. So, you know, if everybody's getting a D or an F, it's usually not the kids' fault. It's usually the way that we're presenting material or assessing them or whatever it is. So we really look at a whole variety of assessments and see how kids are doing and how we can improve to meet the needs of the kids.

Mrs. Nelson viewed student performance on assessments as a signal of how individual teachers, grade levels, and the school overall were doing in terms of fostering student learning. If assessments signaled a problem, she examined what and how teachers were teaching to determine what might be the cause. She considered how teachers might change their approach to certain material to more effectively teach it, or how they might change the assessments themselves to better reflect what students were learning. Because she considered curriculum and instruction, rather than students' deficiencies, as potential contributors to lackluster results, Mrs. Nelson recognized the utility of using assessments as a tool to examine not only student performance, but the other two components of the instructional unit as well. Her examination of teaching and materials helped the teachers to make changes that could lead to more effective teaching and learning.

Student assessment data, then, connected Mrs. Nelson with classroom instruction and served as another tool that framed her interactions with teachers, helping to define leadership practice. For example, problems with test scores sometimes resulted in discussions with teachers about how to improve the instructional program for students. In mathematics, Mrs. Nelson explained that she and the seventh-grade teachers recently addressed a dip in scores.

> I'm very interested in our upper grades, especially our seventh grade. Now they're, you know there's a big jump between being self-contained and being departmental and doing a pre-algebra and that our scores have, over the past couple of years, taken a real dip in seventh grade. And I've talked to the teachers about that, and we've tried to kind of adjust our curriculum and—angled with different groups. And I try to stay on top of things. And, you know, when I see things happening on report cards or something, I try to talk to teachers about what's happening with these kids, how we can assist them.

For Mrs. Nelson, the scores signaled a potential problem with the school's seventh-grade mathematics curriculum. She used the scores to frame a discussion with teachers about how they might change what they were doing in order to improve student learning in mathematics. As a tool, student assessment scores framed and focused the interactions between the principal and teachers. In this way, student achievement data helped to define leadership and management practice at Hillside and served as a lever through which Mrs. Nelson influenced classroom instruction.

Mrs. Nelson used reading assessments for a similar purpose, asking the Curriculum Coordinator to routinely compile students' reading scores for her to review. Mrs. Nelson explained:

> I do receive reports, you know, the reading reports, on a monthly basis on the testing that the classrooms do. End-of-unit, chapter, end-of-cluster tests and so on. . . . I really look at them and see how children are progressing. See if there are some real problems, some things that we really need to look at. Maybe talk to a team about how they feel about a—something that we see that—that I see that maybe is troubling to me. You know, what we're going to do to address this need.

Similar to the standardized test scores in mathematics, for Mrs. Nelson, the reading reports were a key leadership tool; she used them to examine students' progress in reading and to focus discussions with teachers about how they might change their teaching to address students' needs. Consequently, these reading reports, and the discussions they provoked, enabled Mrs. Nelson to connect her work with teachers' classroom practice. Student assessment data were used in a variety of organizational routines, including formal faculty meetings and less formal grade-level meetings.

Typically, however, instead of using test scores to engage in open discussions with teachers, Mrs. Nelson used them as a tool to bring teachers' thinking and practice in line with her own thinking and expectations. Consider, by way of example, one faculty meeting (an organizational routine) during which she reviewed the school's scores on the open-ended questions on the mathematics portion of the Illinois Standards Achievement Test (ISAT).

> As the teachers sat before her, Mrs. Nelson distributed a copy of the scores to each teacher and stood at the front of the room. She explained that these questions are graded in three parts, including "math knowledge, strategic knowledge, and explanation," and that the rubric used to score the test was based on a scale from zero to four. She pointed out that a score of zero means the student "didn't even try" to solve the problem. Referring to her own copy of the scores, she read the results from one of the areas: "44% got a four, 9% got a three, . . . 12% didn't try. . . . We shouldn't have any zeros," she said matter-of-factly. "It is important to encourage them to try and get something down." The teachers were largely silent as they followed along in their own copies of the scores. Mrs. Nelson continued to read the results from the fifth-grade test: "Task 2— different shapes, same area. 23% got a four, and 4% got a three. Fifth-grade teachers, you might want to consider doing a review of geometry in the next week"[4] because there seems to be a weakness in geometry. The fifth-grade team did not appear fazed by her remarks.
>
> After reviewing the results from several additional areas on the test on which students at Hillside and from across the state performed poorly, one teacher raised the possibility that there was something wrong with the test itself because the results did not follow a bell curve. Mrs. Nelson pointed out to her that the ISAT is a criterion-referenced test and said, "There might be something wrong with the way we are teaching!" The teacher replied with emotion, "Something is wrong if everyone in the state is teaching wrong!" Mrs. Nelson explained, "This is a test of higher order skills—a buzz word for the 1990s and 2000s. We want them to explain how they got an answer . . . why this is true. We have to learn how to teach differently. That is why we can't have a lot of ditto sheets. We need to ask questions where they have to write paragraphs and explain their responses."

Finally, toward the end of the meeting, Mrs. Nelson stressed that the teachers should see that their students are familiar with the scoring rubric so that they understand how their answers will be scored. She suggested, "Make a copy of this and have them put it inside their notebook or wherever they keep their math assignments." After fielding a question or two she added, "It's not going to go away, folks."

In this vignette, the test scores framed the interactions between Mrs. Nelson and the teachers. For Mrs. Nelson, test scores offered a glimpse into classrooms that shed light on what students were "getting" and not getting as measured by this particular test. Similar to the writing folders, Mrs. Nelson used student achievement data as an opportunity to bring the teachers' thinking and practice in line with her own expectations and goals for instruction, specifically in terms of content coverage and general pedagogy. By pointing out the fifth grade's weakness in geometry and suggesting that the fifth-grade teachers cover geometry before the next test, she addressed content coverage. By explaining the pedagogical movement in mathematics away from rote learning through "ditto sheets" and toward higher order operations that require students to explain their thinking, and by suggesting that the teachers show students the scoring rubric so that students understand what is expected of them, she addressed general pedagogical approaches in mathematics. Using the student achievement data as a tool, Mrs. Nelson articulated her views of these content and pedagogical issues in an effort to improve instruction at Hillside. This tool helped to shape leadership practice by providing Mrs. Nelson with information with which she attempted to connect with classroom instruction.

From time to time, Mrs. Nelson also participated in routine grade-level meetings, using student achievement data to frame discussions with teachers about instructional improvement at particular grade levels. In the following vignette, Mrs. Nelson attended a fifth-grade team meeting to talk about how the fifth graders had scored on the mathematics portion of the ISAT the previous year:

She read off the breakdown of scores in math and said, "We're below 50% in all those areas." She then urged the teachers to look at the math book they use and to be sure to cover the units that, according to the scores, were causing the most difficulty. "Make sure in the first semester you've touched on all these areas," she told them. She pointed out that *probability* appeared to be a weak area for them and suggested they find some activities they can use to better teach it. She urged them to refer to the Illinois State Goals and also to go to the

Math Resource Teacher to obtain additional classroom resources. When she left the meeting, the teachers responded to her recommendations by planning their upcoming mathematics lessons to include the content Mrs. Nelson suggested they cover. One teacher then heeded her advice by consulting with the Math Resource Teacher and borrowing several materials from her to help with the unit on probability.

This vignette illustrates how student assessment data as a tool framed interaction between Mrs. Nelson and the teachers, defining leadership practice at Hillside. Mrs. Nelson used student test data to frame and focus discussions with teachers about how to change mathematics instruction in order to increase student achievement, in this case urging the teachers to emphasize specific mathematical content on which students were not performing well.

This anecdote, however, highlights an interesting difference between Mrs. Nelson's involvement in efforts to improve writing instruction compared with mathematics instruction. Rather than engaging in a fine-grained analysis of students' work in mathematics (e.g., looking at students' solutions to math problems) similar to her work on students' writing samples, she referred teachers to the Math Resource Teacher for more in-depth help and resources, typically limiting her own involvement in mathematics to issues of content coverage. Mrs. Nelson was more inclined to "get her hands dirty" in students' writing than in their work in mathematics due in part to her training, experience, and self-identification as a reading specialist, her personal emphasis on the importance of good writing, and her recognition of the Math Resource Teacher's many years of experience and expertise in teaching mathematics. The manner in which leadership for instruction at Hillside was distributed across tools *and* people differed depending on the subject matter.

Mrs. Nelson's periodic review of student assessment data with teachers, as part of both formal and informal organizational routines, constituted a boundary practice intended to influence teaching. The student assessment data were tools that enabled Mrs. Nelson to routinely assess and monitor student progress in mathematics and reading. Specifically, they provided her with a window into the classroom and an opportunity to align teachers' thinking and practice with her own expectations for teaching and learning. Occasionally she used the assessment data to press on classroom pedagogy, but more often she used them to press changes in content coverage. Regularly reviewing assessment results with teachers enabled Mrs. Nelson to sustain a connection to classroom practice. This routine, and the tools involved in it (assessment data), helped to define leadership and management practice at Hillside.

Lesson Plan Review Routine

Finally, Mrs. Nelson routinely reviewed teachers' lesson plans in an effort to lead and manage improvement in instruction. The district required teachers to submit lesson plans to school administrators regularly, but Mrs. Nelson transformed this potentially mundane district-mandated organizational routine into a viable connection between her work as a school leader and the teachers' classroom work. One of the school's counselors summed up the lesson plan review routine this way:

> These lesson plans, . . . it's a piece of artwork. It's a craft that these teachers have to do weekly. It's scrutinized, and it's checked. If she comes in the classroom and you are not working on the objective that you said you were going to be working on that day, she wants to know why. I think that's why the school has made its incredible success, because she's there making sure it's going to happen. If it's not going to happen, explain to me why it's not happening. You're not going to sit at your desk crocheting.

Mrs. Nelson took the lesson plan review routine seriously, and sent notes to teachers for plans she believed warranted critical feedback. One teacher who had been teaching at Hillside for 13 years said:

> I think she's come to trust me with my lesson plans. Because she knows I write very prolific ones. In the beginning when I first came here and I wasn't doing them the way she wanted them done, I was getting notes from her quite regularly. I know a lot of the other teachers get notes from her. I have not gotten a note on my lesson plans in years. . . . She sends many notes to many other teachers on their lesson plans. So how involved the notes are, I don't know because I haven't gotten one in years. But I know in the beginning, as I say, the first couple years I came, she was, she, not on me but she did you know, "Gee, what does this mean?" or "Why are you teaching this?" or "What does this key into?" You know, so she was looking at them, you know.

Mrs. Nelson's practice of collecting and reviewing teachers' lesson plans was not just another district paperwork requirement but an organizational routine that enabled her to forge a direct connection to classroom practice. By holding teachers accountable for following their lesson plans and pressing them to explain why they were teaching those lessons, she was able not only to monitor content coverage with respect to the state goals and district frameworks ("What does this key into?"), but also to gauge teachers' understandings of the underlying logic of the curriculum ("Why are you teaching this?").

Because her practice of reviewing lesson plans had become so routine and well defined, the teachers knew exactly what Mrs. Nelson's expectations for their lesson plans were, such as when they were due, what format to use, and what to include in them. Further, they knew that should Mrs. Nelson drop by their classrooms, she expected them to be teaching the lesson plan they had written for that day or, if they were not following their plan, at least to have an explanation for why they were not doing so. This routine enabled Mrs. Nelson to lead and manage instructional improvement across the school. Just like the writing folders and student assessments, the lesson plans were an essential defining element of leadership practice at Hillside, framing and focusing interactions between Mrs. Nelson and the teachers, either face-to-face or off-line. Appropriated as a leadership and management tool, the lesson plans, coupled with Mrs. Nelson's feedback, framed ongoing interactions between the teachers and Mrs. Nelson about classroom instruction.

CONCLUSION

From a distributed leadership perspective, aspects of the situation such as organizational routines and tools are not simply a backdrop or an accessory for school leadership and management practice. Rather, by framing interactions among leaders and followers, organizational routines and tools are a core defining element of that practice. At the same time, organizational routines and tools are a product of practice. For example, while the writing folder review routine shaped leadership and management practice by framing Mrs. Nelson's and the teachers' interactions about writing instruction, it was also the product of that practice in that Mrs. Nelson designed it, as a tool, to reach her goals. Hence, the writing folder review routine both shaped, and was a product of, leadership and management practice at Hillside. Furthermore, the organizational routines and their respective tools—writing folders, student assessment data, and lesson plans—were boundary practices that enabled Mrs. Nelson to span the boundary between leadership and management practice and classroom practice, forging stronger ties to instruction.

The significance of these organizational routines and tools for leadership and management practice at Hillside cannot be overstated. Because the principal and teachers regularly participated in these routines throughout the year, they knew their respective roles and responsibilities when they engaged in the practices. Particularly in the case of the writing folder review and lesson plan routines, teachers knew what Mrs. Nelson expected from them and what they could expect in return in their interactions with her. In this way, routines afforded a certain efficiency in that the principal and teachers knew what to do and did not have to newly construct the norms of interaction every time. Of course, routines also can be inefficient if they become so habitual as to inhibit creative or innovative thinking among organization members.

The three organizational routines discussed in this chapter differed from one another in ways that illustrate how routines and tools as aspects of the situation define leadership and management practice. Specifically, two of the routines were built around existing tools that the school principal appropriated for her own specific purposes, while the third was a routine that she invented. The lesson plans and student assessment data were not unique to Hillside. The school district required administrators at every school to collect lesson plans and to administer a minimal level of student testing. Whereas at other schools administrators might have viewed teachers' lesson plans as just another bureaucratic paperwork requirement, Mrs. Nelson viewed them as a representation of teachers' classroom practices that kept her connected to what teachers were doing and why they were doing it, serving as one basis for her interactions with teachers about instruction. By regularly reviewing the plans and holding teachers accountable to them, she was able to keep a finger on the pulse of instructional practices in every classroom. By redefining the lesson plan routine, assigning to it a meaning that went beyond the typical paperwork requirement, she turned this tool into a leadership and management tool, transforming what could have been a perfunctory district-mandated practice into an organizational routine designed to lead and manage instruction.

Likewise, although the district required every school to administer standardized tests, administrators were not required to use test results as a tool to improve teaching and learning. At Hillside, however, Mrs. Nelson utilized student assessment data to detect potential problems with classroom instruction and curricula, redefining test scores as a key tool to frame interactions with teachers about improving teaching and learning. Further, this tool enabled Mrs. Nelson to shape instructional practices in light of what she perceived was working and not working in classrooms. Similar to the lesson plans, Mrs. Nelson transformed this existing tool—student assessment data—into a tool for leading instruction. These two tools, embedded in organizational routines, forged regular connections between classroom practice and school leadership practice, helping to accomplish functions such as monitoring teaching and learning and forging an alignment between teachers' thinking and Mrs. Nelson's expectations for content coverage and pedagogy.

In contrast to the lesson plans and student assessments, the writing folder review routine was Mrs. Nelson's own creation. Consistent with her belief in the importance of minority students having the ability to write and communicate clearly, she saw a need to improve students' writing at Hillside. To accomplish this goal, she created this routine to ensure that teachers were spending sufficient time on writing in the classroom and to follow students' progress. Although Mrs. Nelson's actions were critical, like the other routines and tools highlighted in this chapter, this leadership practice at Hillside took shape in the interactions between herself, teachers, students, and tools.

The case of Hillside illuminates how school leaders can move beyond the managerial imperative and establish tighter links between school leadership and management practice and classroom practice. By designing organizational routines and appropriating various tools, Mrs. Nelson helped develop leadership and management practice for improving classroom instruction at Hillside. Serving as boundary practices, organizational routines were an efficient means of linking the principal's office with many classrooms on a regular basis.

3

Systems of Practice and Professional Community: The Adams Case

Richard R. Halverson
UNIVERSITY OF WISCONSIN–MADISON

Principal Therese Williams began her principalship in 1989 in a troubled school. Adams School, an urban, public, 1,200-student, K–8 school, ranked among the lowest performing Chicago public schools in student achievement. Adams faculty members, spread across two aging brick buildings, were dominated by social cliques and were unaccustomed to talking about instruction. The declining socioeconomic status of the community contributed to falling expectations about student learning at the school. Dr. Williams was unsure about where to start, but after 10 years of determined effort, she and her leadership team had begun to turn the student-learning story around. When asked about how the change happened, Dr. Williams replied:

> We set the expectation that our school will make progress, and we try to provide the structure, the professional development, the monitoring of instructional program, so that we can reach our goals. We expect to meet our goals, and we set goals that we expect to meet, and excellence has been the standard. We don't accept mediocrity. As an instructional leader here, I would not be comfortable, I would not be satisfied, if our school did not make continual progress. If we don't make the progress we expect to make over a given time, then we are looking at answers and at issues that would probably help us

This chapter was adapted from a previously published article: Halverson, R. (2003). Systems of practice: How leaders use artifacts to create professional community in schools. *Educational Policy and Analysis Archives, 11*(37). Accessible on-line at http://epaa.asu.edu/epaa/v11n37/

to improve. So we don't just sit back with the status quo and say, "That's okay, the staff is happy, the kids are happy." Well I'm not happy, because we are not making progress.

Our research at Adams showed that these expectations not only were shared by the leaders and teachers, but also were "built in" to the school in the form of a powerful professional community among the staff. Dr. Williams stated, "It was only when teachers began to talk with one another about their teaching that the test scores started to rise." Professional community is widely recognized as a valuable quality of schools (Lee & Smith, 1996; Little, 1982; Louis, Marks, & Kruse, 1996; Newmann & Wehlage, 1995). A professional community is shaped around the goals that define teachers as members of a profession dedicated to promoting student learning (Grossman, Wineburg, & Woolworth, 2000). Professional communities develop internal practices and expectations to coordinate the nonroutine nature of teaching practice through self-regulation and the development of information feedback systems (Argyris, 1990; Huberman, 1995; Little & Bird, 1987; Louis, Kruse, & Bryk, 1995). In professional communities, teachers have opportunities to break down the isolation of classrooms in collaborative, problem-setting, and problem-solving activities with colleagues (Halverson, 2002; Hargreaves, 1994; Huberman, 1995; Miller, Lord, & Dorney, 1994; Rosenholtz, 1989b). These activities could include collaborative curriculum design, instructional evaluation, interdisciplinary teaming and curriculum development, textbook and course material review, or school improvement planning (Bryk, Bebring, Kerbow, Rollow, & Easton, 1996). Networks of such activities help to create and sustain the conditions for strong professional communities in schools.

A Consortium on Chicago School Research (1998) report indicated that the component aspects of professional community improved over the years of Dr. Williams's tenure at Adams. By the late 1990s, the Adams community scored high on measures such as a shared focus on student learning, peer collaboration among teachers and leaders, public classroom practices, reflective dialogue among teachers, willingness for teachers to engage in innovation, and schoolwide support for change.

While I knew that a change took place to transform the Adams community, I began my study uncertain of what was responsible for the change. Strong leadership, a determined effort by some faculty, external resources and high-stakes accountability all seemed to have played their part. In my effort to understand the practice responsible for the Adams transformation, I turned to the distributed leadership framework to identify the tools, structures, and organizational routines the Adams staff developed and used. This chapter emphasizes the situational distribution of leadership framework to trace how Dr. Williams and her staff developed and linked a series of programs, or *artifacts*, to reshape the local professional culture to improve student learning. The term *artifact* is used here to describe the programs, policies, or procedures leaders use to influence the practice of others. If artifacts, such as faculty meeting agendas, academic calendars, or professional development plans, are effectively designed and shepherded by leaders in schools, they can give rise to new routines of practice that can reshape the professional culture of a school. Artifacts, then, are the primary tools school leaders use to shape new practices. One mark of successful artifact implementation is the emergence of new organizational routines that can become powerful constituents of a school culture (Halverson, 2004).

Here I will consider how Adams leaders used artifacts to establish powerful organizational routines that reshaped professional discourse at Adams, resulting in the strong sense of professional community that school leaders credited with the improvements in student learning (Halverson, 2002, 2004). The chapter will focus on the development, use, and networking of three key organizational routines: Breakfast Club, a faculty discussion forum; the Five-Week Assessment, a schoolwide formative assessment routine; and the School Improvement Plan, a districtwide annual planning process. Adams staff used these organizational routines to create multiple opportunities for interaction around the key instructional issues of the school. These interactions, over time, helped to create the trust necessary for a powerful professional community focused specifically on literacy instruction in the early grades. Here I tell the story of how these routines came to establish a powerful "system of practice" (Halverson, 2004) that created the capacity necessary for improving student learning.

ADAMS SCHOOL

The Adams School had a long history of service to its neighborhood. An all-White school in the mid-1950s, by 1990 the school consisted entirely of African American students. The academic quality of the school and the socioeconomic status of the students had declined during this demographic transition. By the early 1990s, the local press labeled Adams as one of the 10 poorest, and poorest performing, schools in the city. In terms of the local standardized tests, 78% of students were below national norms in math, and only 15% of students could read at the national norm. After 10 years, Principal Therese Williams and her staff had, by 2000, increased the proportion of students testing at or above the national norms from 22% to 50% in math and from 15% to 33% in reading comprehension on the Iowa Test of Basic Skills (ITBS)(Figure 3.1). These improvements occurred in the face of annual student mobility rates of 30–40% and a 97% low-income

Figure 3.1. Percent of Adams Students at or Above National Norms on ITBS

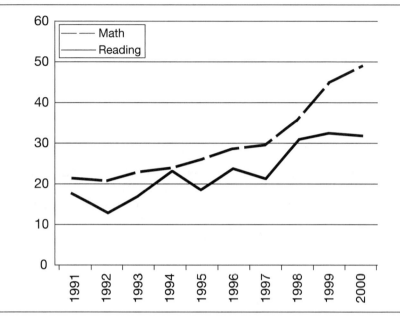

student population. While these gains might look modest by comparison with current NCLB-fueled test score gains, in 2000 these improvements were enough to propel principal Therese Williams and her staff into prominent roles within the district as highly regarded experts on turning around low-performing schools.

The path from leadership to results is often difficult to trace. The Adams staff and school culture underwent a significant change during Dr. Williams's tenure—but which features made the difference in improving student learning? Initially, Dr. Williams felt that integrating research-proven curricula, teaching, and assessment techniques in everyday classroom practice would make the difference. As she explained, "There was a time when we were working very hard, but not working very smart . . . we were not using research to inform our practice, we just kept on reinventing the wheel." Dr. Williams soon found that sharing the research was insufficient to make change. Reinventing the wheel, ironically, turned out to be valuable work because the process of reading and acting together helped to create a strong professional community. Through structured opportunities to review and reflect on research and practice, teachers had to become willing to try out new ideas in their classrooms and, more important, give and receive critical feedback as a staff in order for the instructional changes to take hold. Dr. Williams and her staff began to realize that a strong professional community based on instruction was a necessary condition for using research-driven practices well.

The development of professional community at Adams provides an interesting story of how leaders use artifacts to create new organizational routines. In the initial years of her tenure, Dr. Williams struggled to bring together faculty cliques that fragmented instructional discussions in the school. Several staff members decided to retire or transfer when Dr. Williams arrived. However, Dr. Williams recognized that staff changes were not the answer for improving student learning.

> You can't go in with the idea that you have to get rid of everybody, because you are going to bring in the same kind of problems that are out there. The key is if you have a group of committed people, try to work with them and arm them with the knowledge that they need to become professionals, and I think that is what we try to do also.

To initiate staff interaction, Dr. Williams created frequent school-sponsored opportunities for faculty to interact with one another across peer groups and developed a system of organizational routines that helped teachers interact around instructional issues. Once staff grew accustomed to these interactions, Dr. Williams began to focus discussions around the chronic issues of instruction in the school.

BREAKFAST CLUB

Breakfast Club became the cornerstone organizational routine for the emergent professional community at Adams. Principal Williams and Gwen Tracy, the Adams language arts coordinator, designed the Breakfast Club in 1995 as an opportunity for teachers to discuss research relevant to current instructional initiatives and practices among pre-K–3 language arts teachers. High-stakes district accountability measures had pressured the Adams staff to develop more effective professional training. After several years of mixed results with external interventions to teach best practices, Dr. Williams and her staff began to revise their assumptions about quality professional development. Dr. Williams noted, "We began to believe in the importance of professional community when we realized that, it wasn't taking classes, but that it was when teachers started talking about their teaching that the scores started improving."

Breakfast Club involved monthly meetings in which a teacher led a discussion, before the school day began, about a piece of research, usually concerning reading or writing instruction, with groups of pre-K–3 teachers and administrators. During the years 1998–2001, there were an average of eight Breakfast Club meetings per year, with an average of 14 of the 18 pre-K–3 faculty and staff members in attendance. Principal Williams attended about three-quarters of the Breakfast Club meetings during this period. Hard-learned experience about the perils of imposed professional development opportunities prompted Dr. Williams and Ms. Tracy to build the following features into the Breakfast Club routine:

- The program should not be mandatory, to avoid the stultifying atmosphere of many faculty meetings.
- The substance of the discussions themselves should sell the program—if valued information was exchanged at the meeting, word would get around and people would want to come.
- Meetings should take place in the mornings, so that teachers would be fresh and ready to entertain new ideas.
- Readings should be kept short, so that teachers would have a greater chance of viewing them before coming to the session.
- Teachers should be able to select the readings and lead the discussions.

Dr. Williams thought that a hot breakfast, paid for from her own pocket, would indicate clearly to faculty members that she was willing to sacrifice to get the program off the ground.

Sample Breakfast Club topics from the 1998–2000 school years included a review of a multiple-methods approach to language arts instruction, a conversation about the value and viability of learning centers in primary classrooms, discussions of the components of an ideal language arts classroom, and presentations on how various components of a new schoolwide language arts initiative worked out in teachers' classrooms. The conversations and interactions that started during Breakfast Club have become a significant organizing framework for the kinds of practice that characterize the local professional community. As one first-grade teacher commented after 4 years of participating in Breakfast Club:

We have had it for such a long time that we think it has always been this way, but it hasn't been. It probably started when we started respecting each other and the work that we were doing. . . . Once we started [Breakfast Club] with Ms. Tracy, that was the catalyst. Because teachers presented on different topics, and it's very professional. Our presentations that we put together . . . I mean, not all of them, are better than the ones you go out and pay for.

Although Breakfast Club began as an opportunity for teachers to talk about research and practice, it subsequently evolved into a more complex organizational routine to support teachers' brainstorming, experimentation, and design of curricular initiatives.

Breakfast Club and Professional Community

Dr. Williams and Ms. Tracy originally designed Breakfast Club to involve faculty in discussions of relevant instructional research. However, over time, increased staff participation in Breakfast Club helped to create some of the key characteristics of professional community at Adams, including the establishment of teacher collaboration and curriculum design as cornerstones of the professional development program, the deprivatization of practice, the cultivation and use of in-house expertise among faculty and staff, and the creation of a sense of ownership among staff about the instructional program.

Breakfast Club represented both a change in degree and a change in kind for prior professional development at Adams. Many externally designed professional development efforts, intended to bring new ideas into the school, were perceived as too intermittent and variable in quality to provide much long-lasting impact on student achievement scores. As one teacher described:

A lot of times people come in with a set program, . . . but it did not really help us. It got teachers involved in knowing that you have to use [for example] manipulatives and knowing that quantitatively you could add something to your curriculum. It was fun, and we did it for a while, but it did not help us.

Early in her tenure, Principal Williams organized curriculum review teams, first within grade levels (1990–91) and then across grade levels (1992–93), to get teachers talking about the school's instructional program. Breakfast Club built on and focused this history of teacher collaboration into a routine that supported regular staff discussion of new instructional ideas in relation to current instructional practices within the school. The Breakfast Club routine created systemic opportunities for teachers to reflect on their instructional practices in light of new ideas. Breakfast Club changed the way Adams leaders and teachers thought about professional development in the school; it framed the interactions among teachers and leaders about teacher development differently. Specifically, Breakfast Club encouraged attention to both insider and outsider knowledge. Further, Breakfast Club avoided casting teachers exclusively as learners and afforded them an active, creative position in their own professional development.

The Breakfast Club discussions also helped to deprivatize practice and create in-house instructional expertise. While initial meetings provided opportunities for interested teachers to become familiar with and discuss new ideas, in later meetings teachers reported on their efforts to try out these ideas in their classrooms. Creating a loop within the teacher community, from discussing to experimenting and reporting on their experience with new ideas, helped to create a system of reflective practice in the school. This was particularly true of the teachers who initially took leadership roles in the discussion and experimentation with new language arts ideas and techniques. The reflective loop created by the implementation of Breakfast Club encouraged many teachers to openly discuss language arts instruction with one another. As one teacher articulated:

> Before this, I might have been too nervous to do this [present about my teaching]. But now, when I get in front of the classroom . . . it didn't bother me anymore. Throughout the years, it really makes a difference. Because when you are presenting, when you are talking about that article with your colleagues and they are all accepting you, you realize that this isn't such a bad thing. Before that, when you are closing your doors and nobody is saying anything—you just did your good job and closed your door.

Deprivatizing practice allowed teachers and school leaders to recognize and exploit the considerable local instructional expertise in the design of subsequent professional development opportunities. For example, spin-off routines such as Teacher Leader (established in 1998) provided a half-day professional development meeting to allow teachers to conduct workshops about the ideas developed and shared during Breakfast Club, while Teacher Talk (established in 1997) applied the format of Breakfast Club to the grade 6–8 faculty meetings. The cultivation of in-house expertise, through Breakfast Club and other initiatives, was an important source for developing internal leadership opportunities for teachers within the school. Dr. Williams helped develop organizational routines like Breakfast Club, in part, to provide avenues for fostering both local leadership and instructional expertise, thus helping to enrich the human capital available for subsequent problem-solving opportunities.

A sample Breakfast Club meeting illustrates faculty and staff interaction. During this meeting, a first-grade teacher led a discussion on how to use learning centers to engage some students while others receive instruction directly from the teacher. The tone of the discussion was collegial, with lots of laughter and side conversations as teachers talked with one another about the value of learning centers. The discussion leader commented, "You can't teach the class as a whole. A method won't work if some can read and others are working on the alphabet.... I can't be in two places at one time." A younger teacher expressed her struggle with how to organize a classroom into separate learning areas. Several of the veteran teachers spoke from their experience about developing learning centers. One teacher commented that teachers had to train the students to work separately in learning centers. She explained, "You have to train [the students] to use the learning centers.... You can't do it in the first month of school. It may take 3 to 4 months, but eventually you can send them off." The discussion leader commented that her experience had helped her simplify the process, and she wondered, "Am I getting lazy or am I getting smart?" In previous years she had developed control systems and lots of instructions, forms, and files that generated a lot of paperwork. Now, she was able use a simple system that worked for her. The discussion leader agreed and added, "We as adults have trouble learning to cooperate." Principal Williams quietly observed the discussion and made a point of agreeing with the discussion leader's point that "we should have a half day where we can learn what we are doing in each other's classrooms."

Breakfast Club served as an organizational routine for developing a shared sense of an instructional vision for the school. Instead of mandating a direction for the language arts program, Dr. Williams and Ms. Tracy used Breakfast Club to allow for the collaborative consideration of and experimentation with alternative programs. As teachers explored and reflected upon alternative practices, they came to realize how the proposed practices might remedy the shortcomings of the existing instructional program. In 1999, after several years of discussion and experimentation, the teachers and school leaders selected Pat Cunningham's Four Blocks of Literacy (see Cunningham, Hall, & Defee, 1998) for the cornerstone of their new language arts program. Breakfast Club served as a foundation for teachers to come together on the needs and merits of instructional initiatives, and it provided a structure to support inquiry and collaborative design. The value of Breakfast Club as a forum for reflection on practice was evident as the school community reflected upon its experiences for the purpose of supplementing the initial Four Blocks program. Breakfast Club provided a legitimate, ongoing forum to discuss and yet proposed directions for the instructional program, helping to continually test and revamp the plan for language arts instruction in the school.

FIVE-WEEK ASSESSMENT

The Adams leaders developed Breakfast Club to create an organizational routine for incorporating research into faculty discussions. The successful establishment of Breakfast Club gave rise to a new question: How could

Adams teachers see whether the new practices discussed at Breakfast Club worked in their classrooms? The Five-Week Assessment routine was designed to provide meaningful formative data to teachers and leaders about whether the program initiatives discussed in Breakfast Club improved student achievement on district standardized tests. The culture of professional community and collaborative design, resulting in part from innovations such as Breakfast Club, led Adams school leaders to frame the problem of reshaping the school instructional program in terms of collaborative artifact development—the design and continual redesign of routines and tools to enable instructional improvement.

The Five-Week Assessment offers insight into how the Adams community drew on the capacity developed through Breakfast Club to meet the demands of standardized testing. Faculty discussions of curricular interventions, combined with high-stakes testing expectations, helped create a collective need for a new assessment artifact.

> We realized that the [state] tests themselves didn't give us much information about what we could do to improve our scores—mainly because we received the results well after we could do anything about it. We thought about a more frequent assessment program, say every 5 weeks, that would help us tell where the children were.

The Five-Week Assessment routine design began as an effort to retrofit the specific, learning-outcome demands of the standardized test, particularly in language arts, to the school curriculum. Prior collaborative design efforts suggested that this effort too should provide an occasion for staff collaboration. In 1998, Ms. Tracy and a team of teachers met to design the Five-Week Assessment by undertaking an item analysis of the ITBS exam, focusing on reading comprehension. The design team drew on its experience with reading assessments to assemble a suite of tools teachers could use for a schoolwide assessment of student reading progress. Every 5 weeks, teachers throughout the school conducted the resulting 1–2 hour assessment with their students. The design team collected and graded the assessments, and then discussed the results to plan intervention strategies for underperforming classrooms. The team also developed a plan to move the assessments from reading to other subject areas over subsequent years. Initially designed to prepare students for the ITBS exam, the assessment program shifted toward testing children for the kinds of narrative, expository, and persuasive writing, and open-ended questions required by the new forms of testing developed by the state. Each year, Ms. Tracy presented a monthly schedule for the schoolwide Five-Week Assessments. By 2001, the Five-Week Assessment had become a widely used and discussed diagnostic tool as teachers and leaders anticipated student achievement scores and analyzed their data, through artifacts such as Breakfast Club and Teacher Leader, to shape the existing instructional program and for teachers to check schoolwide student progress.

Five-Week Assessment and Professional Community

While high-stakes accountability policies can provide an occasion to share feedback about the effectiveness of the instructional program, they also can serve to threaten professional community in a school. School leaders who use accountability systems to pit teachers, grade levels, and schools against one another can erode the sense of trust, resulting in a further insulation of practice (see discussion in Chapter 5). At Adams, school leaders realized that using test scores at the classroom level could create competition and resentment among teachers and discourage the formation of professional community. The language arts coordinator commented on the need for grade-level reporting of scores to turn accountability data into a positive force.

> I think . . . when the [standardized test] was first started it did something very interesting that almost forced us to work as a team. . . . [Reporting at the classroom level led us to think] this one teacher over here could be a shining star, but if the other two or three were not getting the same kinds of results then that one teacher didn't look good anymore because my score was not enough to pull up the entire grade level. So, if I want my grade level to get a good score, then I need to help these other teachers pull up to where I am.

The Five-Week Assessment routine helped to mitigate the summative effect of standardized test scores by providing intermittent benchmarks to gauge the projected results. Although the results of the Five-Week Assessment did not accurately predict the standardized test results at first, over time, as the curriculum became more aligned with the assessments, the Five-Week Assessment proved an effective means to point out teachers who were doing particularly well, and served as a warning flag for problem classrooms. For example, in 2000, the Five-Week Assessment revealed that fifth-grade students in a particular classroom were falling behind in science. One teacher commented, "Looking at the Five-Week Assessment saved our butts because we could focus in on helping the students learn the science content they needed to do well on the test." In this case, teachers worked to enhance the existing language arts program with more science-related readings in order to supplement the existing science program. Here, the Five-Week Assessment sounded an alarm to bring Adams resources to bear in addressing instructional issues before they emerged as accountability problems.

While professional community can emerge from the expression and sharing of common interests around instruction, the long-term viability of professional community may well depend on the development of feedback systems to provide information about how collaboratively designed initiatives are working. The Five-Week Assessment routine deepened the professional community by bringing the resources of the community to bear on emergent instructional issues.

SCHOOL IMPROVEMENT PLANNING PROCESS

Unlike Breakfast Club or the Five-Week Assessment, the School Improvement Plan (SIP) was introduced to Adams as a districtwide routine. In many schools, such district-designed instructional planning routines can serve as mandated hoops through which school leaders must jump, completed for the sake of compliance and never consulted until the next round of submission is due, leaving core instructional practices untouched. However, savvy leaders can use routines such as the SIP as opportunities to both satisfy district requirements and create organizational routines that facilitate collective reflection that is shared across the instructional program.

Adams school leaders took the SIP as an opportunity to extend the collaborative design routines established in Breakfast Club and the Five-Week Assessment to develop a comprehensive grasp of the school instructional program. The district-developed SIP routine provided a series of forms and suggested activities designed to help school leaders coordinate budgetary and instructional priorities with the Local School Councils, a school-based decision-making body, and the central office. School improvement planning is intertwined with many of the organizational routines at Adams, reaching back to the arrival of Principal Williams at Adams in the late 1980s. She reported that instructional planning was one of her initial tasks.

> We began school improvement immediately. I believe it was 1988 when the first legislation passed that created School Improvement Plan, and we started from the beginning having everybody who wanted to be involved, involved.

Instructional planning, for Dr. Williams, was a way to get faculty and staff involved in conversations around instruction and its improvement. By the late 1990s, the SIP had come to serve as an umbrella routine to structure school professional development and planning. Each fall, Dr. Williams opened the school year with a review of the student achievement goals as specified in the current SIP. She used the preservice meeting to relate school goals to district goals ("We are not alone. . . . There is a systemwide emphasis on reading instruction.") and displayed an impressive grasp of the details of the Adams instructional plan. For example, in 1999–2000, Dr. Williams described how teachers needed to recommit to teaching phonemic awareness.

> Without direct instructional support, phonemic awareness eludes 25% of in-class first graders . . . imagine the effects it had for our children. As we learned through several Breakfast Club discussions last year, the literature is clear—we can't superficially teach the basics; we must be clear that all students have a firm background.

During the fall semester, teachers participated in the inservice programs through routines such as Breakfast Club, and leaders accessed the progress of instructional innovations through the Five-Week Assessment. During the spring semester, the community revisited the SIP goals and outlined a new plan, during a series of formal meetings, that made up the school improvement routine. In March, specific subject-matter meetings were called to hammer out program priorities and student achievement goals for the upcoming school year. Thus, the final plan submitted in May to satisfy district requirements reflected a school-level adaptation of the SIP routine to cultivate the local development of professional community.

A 2000 SIP meeting on math instruction illustrated how the Adams collaborative-planning process worked. Language arts coordinator Gwen Tracy took the lead by instructing teachers to review the 1999–2000 math plan. After about 5 minutes of buzzing conversation, a first-grade teacher began a discussion of the adequacy of the current textbook series. Ms. Tracy later explained:

> The teachers have to own the meeting process because the SIP depends upon their commitment to the changes we propose. . . . If the teachers don't take charge, the meetings don't work. . . . There were a couple of times during the meeting today where [first-grade teacher Mrs.] Brown looked over at me [for some help at getting the meeting going].

Ms. Tracy related that after many of the early SIP meetings, people would come up to her and request programs or resources they wanted but had not brought up at the meeting. She noted:

> At first, the teachers didn't see it this way; then they realized that all of the resources are passed out through the SIP. If they weren't involved in the process, they didn't get any of the resources.

As the math discussion unfolded, the five members of the Math Team (teachers from grades 1, 3, 5, 6, and 8) coordinated the brainstorming session. One Math Team member noted, "We need to work on the more open-ended, problem-solving aspect of math in anticipation of the new accountability challenges proposed by the ISAT." The eighth-grade Math Team member added, "Next year's [text] book has a lot of practice with open-ended questions. . . . The middle school lessons will have an open-ended question every day . . . consistent with the NCTM1 standards." Teachers' perceptions seemed to be that while the ITBS focused more on testing skills, the new ISAT would focus more on problem-setting and problem-solving issues. The Math Team recognized that the current instructional program was well tailored to the math problems of the ITBS, but was not as well suited to the ISAT.

The meeting served as an opportunity to review previous SIP math plans with respect to other program initiatives. One teacher proposed that the Five-Week Assessment routine in math be expanded to provide the information generated by the language arts assessments: "I think we should make the assessments similar to how they are planned for language arts. I would like to see us plan for the testing in math the same way." This lack of coordination between math and language arts pointed to how the school had chosen to allocate subject-matter organizational resources. Ms. Tracy's role in coordinating the Five-Week Assessment in language arts had no analogue in math—the math exams were developed and conducted by full-time teachers and apparently had not received the same attention and review as the language arts exams. This lack of resources was now being felt as teachers faced the new instructional demands of the ISAT. As one teacher commented, "When you look at last year's ISATs, [you can see] what we are doing now [for the Five-Week Assessments] is not working."

This SIP review and design meeting provided a glimpse into the collaborative design practices at Adams. The meetings were held to provide faculty with an opportunity to shape the school instructional program. The design meetings relied on considerable resources in developing solutions. Prior experiences with the Five-Week Assessment routine, Breakfast Club, and collaborative program design meant that teachers and administrators could focus on program refinement rather than novel redesign; experience with group collaboration practice meant that much of the process simply could be assumed so that participants could focus on how programs could be coordinated into a coherent instructional program rather than on the process of collaboration. As one school leader noted:

> Most of the programs we bring up in the SIP are seeded discussions over lunch and at grade-level meetings. For example, we talked about the Four Blocks program a full year before we introduced it into the

SIP. [One first-grade] teacher who reads a lot presented the basic ideas of the Four Blocks at a Breakfast Club, and there were several Teacher Leader meetings about the Four Blocks program. I know that the program was discussed at grade-level meetings. By the time we talked about putting it into the SIP, everyone was on board.

The School Improvement Plan itself was a district-designed routine that afforded certain forms of school-level planning, coordination with student achievement outcomes, and discretion over resource allocation. In the hands of Adams school leaders, the SIP became an occasion for collaborative design of the school instructional program, and while this practice was not new to the Adams community, the SIP process created a powerful and legitimate routine for school leaders to deepen and extend the collaborative practices that already existed in the school.

The School Improvement Plan and Professional Community

Collaborative inquiry and design are the keys for how the SIP routine established a practice that extended professional community at Adams. While the SIP was itself the outcome of a collaborative design effort, it also served as an "umbrella" routine to coordinate specific instructional planning opportunities throughout the year and as a tool to focus instructional leadership practice across various organizational routines. As an organizing routine, the SIP worked as a powerful hub for focusing professional community in the school.

The SIP provided an ongoing, organizing occasion for collaborative design and assessment of the instructional program rather than an isolated task to be completed and shelved. Comprehensive instructional planning, for Dr. Williams and her co-leaders, was a way to get faculty and staff involved in conversations around instruction. The SIP played a central role in organizing multiple collaborative efforts. As described by one school leader, "Everything is tied into the SIP somehow. That's what gives it credibility in the school." Early on, when the SIP meetings were poorly attended, people would complain about not having the resources to get good work done, and the administrators would reply that the teachers needed to come to the meetings to plan for the things they wanted. "The budget, and the initiatives are all tied in. If you want to participate, you have to come early and stay late [at these meetings]."

Adams leaders set the problem of school improvement planning as a school-level process that addressed the key instructional goals of the school and customized those goals to satisfy the requirements of the SIP. The local emphasis on planning also helped focus the shared instructional vision in the school. The annual Adams collaborative development cycle of the SIP helped ensure that the community at large was involved in both understanding and reviewing the instructional mission of the school.

SYSTEMS OF PRACTICE AND PROFESSIONAL COMMUNITY

Although the value of professional community in schools is widely recognized, knowledge about how to create and sustain professional communities is not as widely understood. Grossman, Wineburg, and Woolworth's (2000) experience with developing professional community in a high school led them to comment:

> We have little sense of how teachers forge the bonds of community, struggle to maintain them, work through the inevitable conflicts of social relationships, and form structures for social relationships over time. Without such understanding, we have little to guide us as we create community. (p. 6)

We do have some understanding, however, of what leaders do in schools with strong professional communities. Louis, Kruse, and Bryk (1995) conclude that the most important task for school leaders is to create meaningful opportunities for teachers across the school to work together on pressing issues of common interest. Other key behaviors include being physically present in the school, creating networks of conversation among faculty, making resources available to support individual teacher development, building bridges and networks to practice and knowledge outside the local school, and fostering a school community in which instruction is viewed as problematic.

In many cases, these behaviors both lead to and require structural supports for successful results. Making successful leadership practice accessible means, in part, creating representations of practice that go beyond how leaders create structures to get at how these structures "hang together" in practice. If we assume that professional community is an effect of how these behaviors together shape a school culture, then we are faced with the need to develop both conceptual tools and practical examples that simultaneously demonstrate how behaviors support one another and how aspiring leaders can fashion similar systems in their schools. The knowledge garnered needs to integrate what is known about the *what* of professional community with frameworks to show *how* networks of practice can be developed to support such practices.

A distributed perspective on leadership helps to identify and understand the practice that establish the conditions of professional community in schools. A distributed perspective defines instructional leadership as the establishment and maintenance of the conditions for improving teaching and learning in schools. Taking a distributed leadership perspective means focusing on leadership practice and the *tasks that make up this practice.* These tasks are distributed across two primary dimensions in schools: the social distribution and the situational distribution. The *social distribution* refers to the network of people engaged in leadership tasks, while the *situational distribution* refers to those aspects of the situation that frame the interactions among these people, and concerns how activities are enabled and constrained by the context within which people work (Spillane, Halverson, & Diamond, 2001).

The Adams case suggests that professional community is an outcome of certain configurations of social networks in a school. Leaders influence the development of social networks not only through direct participation, but also indirectly through the design and implementation of organizational routines. Breakfast Club, for example, was a routine designed to allow for faculty interaction around literacy research. When taken together, the routines at a given school compose a *system of practice* that coordinates the practice of the school's instructional program. A system of practice describes how the local network of routines and tools facilitates the flow of the instructional practices of the school. Teachers and school leaders not only work within the constraints of the network of routines in their given situation, but think about the limits and possibilities of their practice in terms of this network. Changing the range of available instructional artifacts not only changes the context of learning, but also can influence the ways that teachers understand learning in their classrooms. At Adams, the Five-Week Assessment is best seen as a consequence of Breakfast Club that amplified the professional community already established and focused faculty collaboration into new areas of assessment. A system of practice perspective suggests that, in order to understand the function of any given routine, it is best to view how the routine both relies on and enables other routines in the system. Organizational routines, then, result from behaviors guided and constrained by other routines over time. A large part of leadership agency involves coordinating and maintaining organizational routines and tools in order to create desired outcomes.

Professional community, I suggest, is an outcome of certain systems of practice in schools organized around sharing and developing instructional expertise and practice. Researchers have understood the development of strong professional community in a school as an enhancement of the school's capacity to engage in instructional improvement (Youngs & King, 2000). One way to understand professional community as a form of capacity is to treat it as a special kind of social capital. Coleman's (1988) concept of social capital refers to resources available to an actor or an organization by virtue of participation in certain interpersonal or institutional structures. While material and human capital are possessed by the actor personally, social capital "inheres in the structure of relations between actors and among actors" (p. 98). Social capital is developed through social interactions that build trust (Wehlage, 1993). Coleman describes trust as accumulated through participation in networks of obligation and commitment, which offer opportunities for participants to rely on one another for the pursuit of common interests or for the completion of tasks. At Adams, Dr. Williams's work developing Breakfast Club aimed to create a new form of professional interaction around literacy practices. Networks of reciprocal obligations and commitment develop trust and reputation in an organization (Fowler, 1999).

Professional trust is developed as actors realize they can share ideas with colleagues, and reputation accrues when actors develop opinions about the trustworthiness of other actors. Bryk and Schneider (2002) suggest that a high level of trust among adults in schools is a critical resource for school leaders engaging in program reform. In their examination of Chicago Public School data from 1990 to 1996, they found that schools with high levels of trust at the beginning of reform efforts had a 1 in 2 chance of improving student achievement scores in math and reading, while schools with low levels of trust faced a 1 in 7 chance of making significant gains. While the cause-and-effect relationship of trust and change is difficult to trace, this research points toward how trust can be used as a key resource for school leaders in making organizational change.

Professional community, then, is a kind of social capital that emerges in certain systems of practice. To create professional community, school leaders either shape existing routines or design new routines to create the structures that foster social capital. Coleman (1988) describes how social capital develops through the closure of social or information structures in organizations. Closure happens when actors have opportunities to interact, create trust, and develop reputations around selected practices. Closure involves completing feedback loops for information and social interaction in organizations. Social capital is developed in organizations and interactions that present redundant opportunities for closure. Open systems, on the other hand, have few structured opportunities for closure. In open systems, actors diverge from the source of information or directive without structured opportunities for subsequent reconvergence. Trust around core practices does not develop because actors have little opportunity to enter into relations that create obligations or commitments. Many school instructional systems of practice are open in this fashion (Figure 3.2). In order to promote professional communities in schools, leaders must create legitimate structures that give rise to the occasions in which teachers can share and reflect upon their hard-won instructional expertise, question their own practice, and accept the sugges-

Figure 3.2. Generic Open School Model

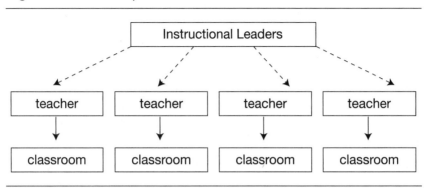

tions of peers. Closing a system means establishing routines that close feedback loops in which actors can receive information about the degree to which obligations have been entered into and fulfilled.

PROFESSIONAL COMMUNITY AND THE CLOSURE OF OPEN SYSTEMS AT ADAMS

School leaders at Adams helped establish routines that give teachers opportunities to discuss practice, develop programs, and understand assessment information. These routines helped to create the kind of trust within the organization that in turn fosters the possibility for professional community. To highlight features of how local leaders influenced the system of practice, I consider how Adams leaders and staff implemented the three routines discussed above to shape the professional interaction in the school and nurture practices that resulted in a strong professional community.

School leaders at Adams used organizational routines to help teachers engage in conversations to improve teaching practice. As routines such as Breakfast Club and the Five-Week Assessment gave rise to new routines that began to reshape professional interaction at Adams, the emerging sense of professional community in turn inspired and led to the design of new routines. In other words, professional community became a form of organizational capacity that served as a condition for emergent routine and tool design efforts. This section outlines how each routine created the social capital of professional community within the school, and discusses how the routines together helped to form the backbone of a reformed system of practice at Adams.

Each of the routines described above provided closure at a different level of the social system at Adams. Breakfast Club, for example, provided a forum for teachers to reflect with one another both on research and on one another's practice (Figure 3.3). As it grew to maturity, Breakfast Club added a collaborative design dimension as a platform for the development and customization of the school language arts program. The communication network among teachers sparked by Breakfast Club created multiple opportunities for interaction around instruction, planning, and assessment among teachers and school leaders. Much of the social capital developed during Breakfast Club stemmed from the conscious effort of school leaders to encourage teachers to take leadership roles in conducting and participating in meetings. The status of Breakfast Club within the school community gave leaders a forum within which to shape the school's instructional improvement agenda.

While administrators conducted informal and formal assessments of classroom teaching, the system of practice included no legitimate structures (other than personal invitation or relationship) for teacher observation of other classrooms. Interaction in Breakfast Club consisted of self-reports of what teachers did in their classrooms. The Five-Week Assessment routine helped to close a loop in the instructional system by providing measures for how well teachers were implementing the innovations discussed during Breakfast Club (Figure 3.4). The Five-Week Assessment provided another chance for professional interaction as teachers collaboratively developed and analyzed measures of classroom-level student achievement. The production and discussion of customized quantitative feedback helped to create professional obligations among staff. The collaborative development and implementation of the Five-Week Assessment provided needed closure among teachers about whether instructional innovations were working. The Five-Week Assessment

Figure 3.3. How Breakfast Club Closes the System of Practice

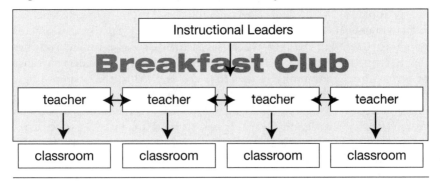

Figure 3.4. How the Five-Week Assessment Closes the System of Practice

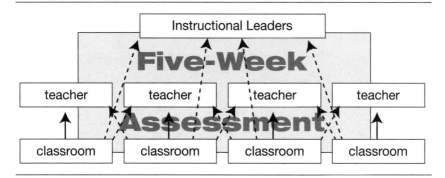

also gave school leaders feedback on how instruction fared in classrooms. Incorporating Five-Week Assessment data into Breakfast Club discussions helped to preserve the tipping point (Gladwell, 2000) at which the professional community could sustain self-reflective assessment practices without imploding or becoming irrelevant.

Finally, the School Improvement Planning routine augmented the Adams professional community by establishing opportunities for teachers and school leaders to articulate what they had done and to build this into the schoolwide instructional plan. Since the school was accountable to the district and to the Local School Council for achieving the SIP goals, the collaborative-planning process provided sanctioned space for staff interaction to determine the direction for the instructional program. Adams leaders and staff created committees, meeting schedules and agendas, and stipends to establish the SIP activities as an organizational routine for staff interactions (Figure 3.5). These meetings created obligations among community members to draft and implement viable plans; the successful completion and execution of the plans created trust among members that their work was not in vain.

Separately, the Adams routines described here provided structures for interaction that supported the creation of certain kinds of obligations around instructional issues. Analyzing the function of each routine in isolation, however, misses the systemic nature of the way professional community has evolved at Adams. A school improvement plan, for example, creates neither an atmosphere of innovation nor the means for formative and periodic assessment of practice. Similarly, a 5-week assessment that attempts to measure teacher instructional performance progress alone can splinter professional communities because of the threat that comparing teachers with one another

Figure 3.5. How the School Improvement Plan Closes the
System of Practice

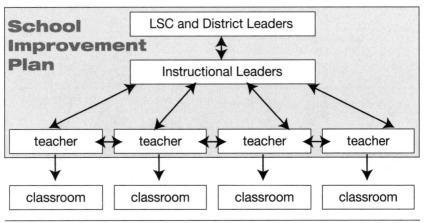

will make them less likely to collaborate on instructional matters. Together, however, these routines help to create a coherent system of practice that brings closure for several different opportunities for faculty interaction (Figure 3.6). The Adams professional community is the product of these aggregated organizational routines. Considered as a system of practice, the routines and tools described here relied on one another as conditions for design and as resources for subsequent design and problem-solving efforts.

Several interesting issues arose in this analysis of practice, tools, routines, and professional community. Did the Adams routines rely on or create professional community? It might be argued that there was a strong pre-existing sense of professional community at the school upon which these routines depended for their subsequent success in framing instructional practice. Bryk and Schneider (2002) suggest that existing high levels of trust provide a key resource for leaders in facilitating school change. There seems to have been a strong sense of community and shared vision among a tight group of leaders at the school who perceived their responsibility to improve student learning in the school. Perhaps there was an already existing strong sense of professional community among these teachers that, when tapped by designed routines, blossomed into schoolwide professional community. If professional community can be measured in terms of student learning, however, the effects of the pre-existing professional community were not supported by increases in student test scores. Indeed, in the early 1990s, Adams ranked among the poorest performing schools in the district. One administrator recalled that, before Principal Williams, there were strong teachers in the

Figure 3.6. How the Routines Taken Together Close the System of Practice

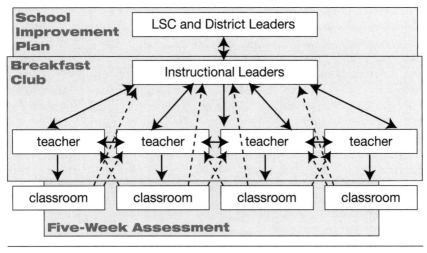

school and a strong sense of social community among teachers and leaders, but that teachers who initiated discussions about instructional issues felt stigmatized and silenced.

While the model provided here cannot conclusively demonstrate causality between organizational routines and professional community, it does suggest that the routines developed by Dr. Williams and her leadership team were key instruments to create trust and open discussions of instructional practice among teachers. The routines themselves, however, do not seem to be easily separable from the context in which they were created. Anecdotal evidence that other schools that experimented with Breakfast Club-like routines felt little impact on the development of professional community suggests that the routines themselves are not the answer. Rather, it is how the routines interacted with one another, creating possibilities that afforded redundant opportunities for professional interaction, that seems to account for the strong professional community at Adams. Further investigation is required into schools just embarking on the creation of professional community as an avowed outcome to explore the relation between routine construction and the underlying forms of human and social capital that make professional community possible.

Does reliance on the analysis of routines as the path to professional community give short shrift to the importance of interpersonal and spiritual leadership practice in schools? This analysis is certainly not intended as a comprehensive approach to understanding school leadership practice. Routines merely establish the conditions for practice in organizations—the actual practices of teaching and learning involve levels of agency well beyond the determining structures of routines and tools. The moral leadership and interpersonal skills required to build consensus, establish vision, and give hope in schools transcend the structural components of the instructional context. Still, organizational routines provide powerful tools and symbols to convey moral and interpersonal leadership, and the system of practice establishes the conditions for interaction that shape the school's culture. The ability of leaders to create routines that alter the existing system of practice in schools is a powerful capacity not only for shaping the traditions of teaching and learning but also for providing inspiration through symbolic leadership. The analysis of the routines that compose the system of practice by itself may not tell the whole story of instructional leadership, but it does point to a valuable place to start making successful leadership practice accessible to interested others.

CONCLUSION

This case of how a system of designed and implemented routines helped to create a vibrant professional community at Adams provides a vantage point for understanding the nature of professional community in the school. The case shows how Adams leaders exercised agency in designing and adapting organizational routines to shape professional community. Leadership practice is constituted in part by the ways leaders seek to redesign and manipulate organizational routines. Taken together, these routines help to enable leadership practice around particular tasks, which create and sustain the occasion for directed and purposeful interactions among staff.

While many schools offer ample opportunities for interaction, not all of these interactions help create professional community. Grossman, Wineburg, and Woolworth (2000) suggest that when conversations around instruction occur in schools with high levels of social capital but no significant history of professional community, a sense of "pseudocommunity" is created in which actors may interact but do not engage in difficult discussions about instruction. In such schools, there are few structured opportunities for interaction about the quality or the process of instruction, and thus little social capital is developed around instruction. The Adams case demonstrates how leaders created organizational routines to address what they perceived to be the chronic instructional issues of the school, and then leveraged the capacity developed by prior routines to create new routines that deepened and enriched the school's professional community. Mapping the routines that local leaders created and adapted to shape instruction provides an important way to understand the development of professional community. Identifying what the key routines are and understanding the ways they fit together in practice offer insight into the kinds of situational constructs local leaders build and rely on in developing local professional communities in their schools.

Appendix 3.1. Adams Organizational Routines

Artifact	Purpose	Description	Designers	Duration of Service
1. Breakfast Club	To provide in-house professional development for and by Adams faculty	Monthly meetings before school at which faculty members make and discuss presentations on research relevant to current instructional programs	Language Arts Coordinator, Principal, Teachers	1995–present
2. School Improvement Plan (SIP)	To create annual local school plan to align instructional and budgeting priorities for the upcoming school year	District-designed artifact that acts as a catalyst for local planning efforts as leaders and teachers develop instructional program to meet mandated student test performance targets	District, Principal, Administration, Teachers (approved by Local School Council)	1989–present
3. Five-Week Assessment	Locally designed testing program to provide formative data to complement summative standardized testing data	Testing program based on reverse engineering summative tests to give teachers and leaders a sense of progress toward improved standardized test achievement	Language Arts Coordinator, Assistant Principal, Principal, Teachers	1995–present
4. Teacher Observation Process	Process to provide formative and summative evaluation of teachers according to union guidelines and district policies	District and locally designed forms used to make sense of principal's teacher observation session; evaluations based on district guidelines and local instructional program priorities	District, Principal, Assistant Principal	1989–present

Artifact	Purpose	Description	Designers	Duration of Service
5. Real Men Read	Annual event designed to bring male African American role models into the school to read to students	An annual school-wide breakfast program in which African American men gather to eat and read to children throughout the school	Language Arts Coordinator, Assistant Principal, Principal	1998–present
6. Career Day	Annual event designed to offer Adams students an opportunity to survey career possibilities	A two-part annual assembly for middle school students to listen to African American speakers, then meet with African American professionals in a variety of career fields	Guidance Counselor, Principal, Teachers	1999–present
7. Chicago Annenberg Challenge Curriculum Planning Process (CAC)	Year-long curriculum planning process to document collaborative design efforts in building multi-disciplinary curricula	Collaborative curriculum design effort using LeTUS project-based science curricula as a seed for building middle school cross-disciplinary curricula	Science Coordinator, Teachers, Northwestern and Roosevelt University Researchers	2000–2001
8. Science Coordinator Position	Position established to design science program for Adams's designation as Math-Science Academy	Promotion of 6th-grade teacher Tim Zacharias to renovate science program and to design and teach middle school science curriculum in collaboration with classroom teachers	Science Coordinator, Principal, Assistant Principal	1999–2000

Appendix 3.2. Design Cycle Analysis Model

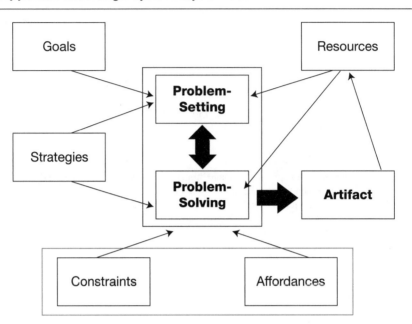

Source: Halverson, 2002

4

Cultivating High Expectations in an Urban Elementary School: The Case of Kelly School

John B. Diamond
HARVARD UNIVERSITY

> I have high expectations for the [children]—I've said to the staff and I'm sure they agree . . . there are no excuses. In the past there have been excuses why children, especially inner-city children, don't do well. Because they come from disadvantaged homes and what have you. Well, we can't do anything about that and I've said to [teachers] over and over, "Parents send the best they have. They don't keep the good ones at home." So we have to work with what we have and do the very best job that we can do.
>
> —Dr. Johnson, Kelly School's Principal[1]

As Dr. Johnson sees it, she is working to ensure that students at Kelly School, a 100% African American K–8 school in Chicago, acquire a strong academic foundation, develop self-esteem, and reach their full academic potential. She argues that "the teachers here, the entire staff, we want these children to succeed, so we try to do the things to help them succeed." While she works in an inner-city school in a low-income African American neighborhood, she argues that "there are no excuses" for students not to excel academically. Instead, she believes that it is the responsibility of the teachers and the administration to ensure students' success. Based on test scores, she and her colleagues have demonstrated impressive outcomes. Over the past several years, students' test scores have improved dramatically. In 1995, 26% of students met or exceeded national norms on the Iowa Test of Basic Skills (ITBS) in English and 40% did so in mathematics. By 2002, those numbers had skyrocketed to 72% and 69%, respectively. This is remarkable especially when compared with overall district test scores. The 2002 figures on the ITBS for the district are 43.2% at or above national norms for reading and 46.9% for mathematics, which means that Kelly substantially outperforms the district as a whole. Raising expectations for students and increasing teachers' accountability for student learning were two important components of this success, according to school leaders.

Teachers hold lower expectations for African American students and students from low-income families when compared with White students and students from more affluent backgrounds (Diamond, Randolph, & Spillane, 2004; Ferguson, 1998). These lower expectations can be a major barrier to school improvement in schools serving a large percentage of African American students from low-income families. Therefore, a critical component of leadership in urban schools involves attending to teachers' expectations for their students. In this chapter, I use a distributed perspective to examine how leaders at Kelly School worked to raise teachers' expectations for low-income African American students and increase teachers' sense of responsibility for student learning. In doing this, I map some of the organizational routines associated with these efforts and discuss how leadership is stretched over people and tools in the execution of these routines.

BUILDING TEACHERS' EXPECTATIONS FOR STUDENTS

Teachers tend to have lower expectations for working-class African American students than they have for middle-class White students (Ferguson, 1998; Lee & Smith, 2001). Low teacher expectations can have a negative impact on student learning by leading teachers to give students less challenging coursework and by leading students to work less diligently on academics, falling in line with teachers' low expectations (Diamond et al., 2004). These expectations are especially influential for the academic achievement of African American students, who may be influenced more powerfully by teachers' expectations for them (Ferguson, 1998).

Teachers' expectations also can be studied as an organizational phenomenon through the analysis of teachers' sense of responsibility for student learning (the extent to which teachers feel responsible for what students learn) (Diamond et al., 2004). While current popular educational discourse advocates the stance that "all children can learn," teachers' personal responsibility for student learning varies across schools. In some schools, "teachers take personal responsibility for the success or failure of their own teaching" (Lee & Loeb, 2000, p. 8). In others, teachers blame students and families for low student performance. In contexts high in teacher responsibility, teachers internalize responsibility for students' learning, adjust their instructional practices to meet students' needs, and have a high sense of efficacy around their teaching (Lee & Smith, 2001). While research suggests that high expectations and teachers' sense of responsibility for student learning are associated with improvements in student performance, we know very little about how to build these characteristics among teachers. How do school leaders cultivate high expectations and sense of responsibility for student learning in the context of low-income urban schools? The next section briefly discusses the distributed leadership perspective, which I will use to analyze this process at Kelly School.

THE DISTRIBUTED PERSPECTIVE: EXAMINING MACROFUNCTIONS, MICROTASKS, AND ORGANIZATIONAL ROUTINES

The distributed perspective provides a conceptual framework for examining how school leadership and management unfolds through the day-to-day actions of school leaders. From a distributed perspective, instructional leadership is an interactive relationship among leaders, followers, and the situation. At the core of the distributed perspective is a focus on leadership and management tasks. These tasks can be divided into macrofunctions (e.g., selling an instructional vision, monitoring instruction, and building norms of trust, collaboration, and academic press) and microtasks or routines that enable the accomplishment of the broader goals. By focusing on the enactment of leadership and management microtasks and organizational routines, we are able to decouple leadership practice from the individual leader and examine how it is a product of a constellation of leaders and followers working within organizational contexts.

In this chapter, I focus on two important macrofunctions: *constructing and selling a vision of high expectations for students* and *building accountability for students' outcomes among teachers*. I argue that these functions were addressed at Kelly, at least partially, through a set of related routines. First, in order to support the vision of high expectations for students, school leaders at Kelly worked to cultivate a formal and informal discourse that reinforced high expectations for students. The task of cultivating these expectations was stretched across multiple leaders, routines, and tools in ways that reinforced high expectations within the school setting. Second, in order to create a sense of responsibility for students' outcomes among teachers, school leaders used a designed tools (a "skill chart") and a formal discourse of teacher accountability in the context of formal leadership settings. In this case, leadership also was stretched across people and aspects of the situation.

DEFINING INSTRUCTION

The distributed perspective emphasizes the importance of exploring relations between leadership and managment practice and instruction. In this discussion, instruction is viewed as constituted in the interaction among teachers, students, and materials (Cohen & Ball, 1998). Therefore, teachers' expectations for students are an important issue for instructional leadership and instructional practice. Teachers' expectations for students influence their teaching strategies, the instructional content that they present to students, and their own sense of whether or not their efforts as teachers make a difference (Diamond et al., 2004). Research demonstrates that when teachers doubt their students' intellectual capacity, they treat students differently during classroom interactions and give students less-challenging coursework. Other research shows that teachers' expectations can be coupled with their own sense of responsibility for what students learn. When teachers doubt their students' capability, they are less likely to adjust their instructional practices to meet students' needs (Diamond et al., 2004). Therefore, building high expectations for students is an important, although often overlooked, mechanism through which leaders can influence instruction.

STUDYING EXPECTATIONS

The data for this chapter were collected as part of the distributed leadership project discussed in Chapter 1. For the present chapter, I analyzed data from teacher and administrator interviews and from observations in formal settings (e.g., classrooms, faculty meetings) and informal settings (e.g., teacher lunch periods) at Kelly Elementary School. I focused on teachers' and administrators' discourse about students, families, and the external community, and the ways in which teachers' beliefs were conveyed through social interaction both with their colleagues and with students and parents. I also analyzed teachers' instructional practices through classroom observations and teachers' self-reports in order to capture the extent to which teachers felt responsible for student learning.

Data from research during 2 academic years included interviews with 11 members of the 22-person staff, 27 formal meeting and classroom observations, and 24 informal observations (lunch meetings, hallway conversations). In addition to these data, I had many informal conversations with teachers, administrators, and support staff about the school, students, families, and community. All of these observations resulted in the production of typed field notes. The data were analyzed to capture teachers' and administrators' beliefs about students, families, and communities; teachers' expectations and sense of responsibility for student learning; and leadership and managment practices designed to influence teachers' beliefs about students and sense of responsibility for student learning.

KELLY SCHOOL

Kelly School is located in a predominantly (90%) African American and low-income neighborhood in Chicago in which over 55% of school-aged children are from families living below the federal poverty line (Correa, Easton, Johnson, Ponisciak, & Rosenkranz, 2004). The community is a collection of contrasts. It includes public housing apartments, abandoned lots, and a few commercial buildings, on the one hand, and an elementary school, high schools (three are located in a two-block radius), and a small number of newly constructed condominiums, on the other. It also is located near a major expressway and not far from a university campus and a community college. Outsiders hold negative perceptions of the neighborhood. However, many of the long-time community residents and parents who volunteer at the local schools have a long history of activism and feel a strong connection to their community. They recognize the neighborhood's challenges but hold on to its potential.

In the 2 years I spent at Kelly, the challenges of the community rarely impacted the largely tranquil school environment. In fact, while the school had a "security guard" stationed at the front door, she was an older, very frail African American woman who was nodding off about half the time I entered the building. Her narcoleptic pattern, combined with the fact that major problems rarely were visible or discussed, suggested that her presence was as much a formality as a necessity.

The student population in 2001 was 100% African American, over 90% of the students received free or reduced-price lunch (representing an increase since 1995 when 82% of students received free or reduced-price lunch). While this is a high percentage of low-income students, there is a range in the income level and resources possessed by students' families. For example, based on observations of parent–teacher conferences, parents in the hallways, as well as teacher reports, it is clear that the parents come from a range of backgrounds and occupational categories. Many parents work in civil service jobs (e.g., post office or police department). As the school's fifth-grade teacher

Ms. Grant put it, the parents are "low to middle income. Most of the parents have blue-collar positions. I don't know any that have a corporate background. . . . A third of my class' parents work at the post office." A few of the students are children of the school's teachers, including Ms. Grant's daughter who attended the preschool program. This suggests that at least some teachers are very comfortable with the school's educational program.

Still, public perception of the neighborhood (and by association, the school) is not good. Administrators discuss the challenges, for example, of recruiting quality teachers to the school because of the image of the surrounding community. The principal explained:

> Because of our location in the city, we're in an urban setting . . . we have the highest percentage of teacher vacancy [among the city's subdistricts]. I have two subs on my staff that have been here since the beginning of the school year. . . . I think there's a teacher shortage, period, but in this region it is extremely difficult because . . . it has a reputation. Sometimes I wonder about that because the things that happen here [happen] all over the city. . . . Staffing is always a problem to get teachers, qualified teachers, and teachers who want to come to the school, that's the problem. The ones that have come here, some might have been resistant initially, but once they get here they find it is a very nice school and all the preconceived notions that they may have about a school . . . fade away very quickly.

One of the teachers, Ms. Whitten, shared how she came to teach at the school. Her experience provides an excellent example of how public perceptions of the community influence teachers' perceptions of the school and how the school environment can help overcome these negative perceptions.

> I had no intentions of transferring to this school because I lived in the South suburbs. And the [technology coordinator] and [the principal] . . . kept calling me at home, leaving these messages: "Come over to the school." So one day I said, "Okay, I will go over to this school," and since they started at 7:45 I thought, "I'll go over there and I can still get to my school, you know, by 9:00 at the latest." I thought, "I'll go over there, listen to them and that'll be that." I said, "I'm not transferring." And I tell people this story all the time. I said, "I'm driving down [the] street and I'm going, [the technology coordinator] has lost her mind if she thinks I'm coming over in this neighborhood to work." I'm looking at garbage and trash and crack-heads, you know, at seven something in the morning. I said, "No way am I going in this area to teach." . . . I came into the building and you could just

feel the difference. . . . And I could just, I could just feel it. And when I met the kids . . . I'm going, "There's really something going on here." And by the time I left, (she laughs) I had signed transfer papers.

As Ms. Whitten's comments suggest, Kelly has a welcoming feel. In a certain sense, it is an island in an otherwise difficult neighborhood. When walking into the school, one is always greeted warmly. It is a small school, fewer than 300 students, so it does not take much time to get to know all of the teachers and administrators and to recognize students. All of the classrooms are located on two hallways. The first floor has pre-K through third-grade classrooms, and the second floor has fourth through eighth grades. There is one classroom per grade level. The hallways are quiet throughout much of the day, until lunch hours, when students can be heard talking loudly in the lunchroom, which is located in the basement next to the teachers' lounge. There is always laughter during staff meetings and informal interactions. This contributes to a school environment in which teachers, administrators, and students seem very content.

THE PRINCIPAL: DR. JOHNSON

In many ways, the Kelly philosophy is an extension of its principal, Dr. Johnson. She has worked in the Chicago Public Schools for 30 years in administration at the district and school levels and is in her early 50s. The oldest of four children from a middle-class African American neighborhood on the South Side of the city, she has always felt responsibility and affection for younger people. As she explains, "I've always sort of been drawn to children. I was the oldest in the family. . . . There were four of us and I was responsible when my parents were working. . . . I was responsible for seeing after the other three, and . . . I'm still working with children."

A product of the Chicago Public Schools, Dr. Johnson is a tall, thin, brown-skinned African American woman with dark brown hair. She dresses impeccably and expects professional dress among her staff. Jeans are not considered proper attire for Kelly's teachers.

Dr. Johnson's leadership, and that of the teachers and other administrators at Kelly, reinforces teachers' responsibility for students' performance. As one of the school's key leaders, Dr. Johnson embeds her leadership work in a keen awareness of the larger social forces aligned against her students. She believes that because most of her students come from low-income families, their homes may contain fewer educational resources than more affluent households. However, when asked about her students' potential for academic success, she argues passionately, "They can do it." She places a great weight on her educational mission, insisting that her school must meet the needs of its students because, as she says, "they're building more and more institutions to incarcerate people, and they're just waiting for some of our brightest." Her comments and actions place the onus for student learning on the school, and, along with her colleagues, she engages in multiple practices to reinforce this perspective among others in the school. While Dr. Johnson is a focal point of this discussion, this chapter utilizes the distributed perspective to discuss leadership activity at Kelly and how it is enacted. It is therefore not the story of an individual leader working in isolation but of leadership and management that takes shape in the interaction of people as mediated by aspects of their situation.

CREATING A CULTURE OF HIGH EXPECTATIONS

High Expectations in Formal Routines

Student achievement is highly valued at Kelly. The school's public spaces are filled with students' work, and the students' academic performance is praised by the posting of test scores and other student accomplishments in the hallways and in the main office. Students' academic performance is a constant point of discussion at Kelly. In the spring of 2000, the test score results were posted in the main office, and several teachers, the principal, and the assistant principal informed me about the results at the beginning of our conversations.

The demographic backgrounds of many of the children at Kelly often are associated with low levels of student achievement. For example, the majority of the children come from low-income homes located in an economically impoverished urban neighborhood. Nonetheless, teachers and administrators stress that these background characteristics must not be used as excuses for lowered expectations. For instance, the principal argues that teachers need to proactively address whatever challenges students might have. Dr. Johnson explains:

> We have to just jump in with our kids. We just can't—we have to—
> because maybe in some other kids, White schools, maybe their
> experience, [their] background at home might be a little different and
> even in many Black schools in different communities where parents
> take more time, they're involved [with] their children, they're in-
> volved in activities. They get the kind of exposure maybe our children
> might not get. So, therefore, we just have to jump right—they can do
> it, you just have to . . . jump right in and do it.

Three interrelated organizational routines were used to reinforce high expectations for students' performance and to build a strong sense of responsibility for student learning among teachers. First, the entire staff met weekly for 90-minute professional development sessions devoted to substantive instructional issues. Within these meetings, a formal discourse emphasizing students' capacity for high achievement was reinforced. Second, school leaders created a tool and routine, the skill chart, that allowed them to monitor classroom instruction and student skill mastery in ways that enhanced their efforts to influence teachers' instructional practices. More specifically, the skill chart was a document (filled out by teachers) that linked teachers' lesson plans with state and district standards, key skills assessed on the Iowa Test of Basic Skills, and each individual student's mastery of those skills. Using this skill chart, school leaders sought to reinforce the belief that student achievement was directly linked to teachers' instructional practices. This message was reinforced often during professional development meetings. In addition to these first two formal routines, an informal discourse was cultivated that reinforced among adults the belief in students' capacity for high achievement. Finally, a set of cultural relevance (Ladson-Billings, 1994) organizational routines combined a daily morning ritual, displays of students' work, and culturally relevant symbols and activities designed to build students' self-esteem and their belief in their own capacity for high achievement.

High Expectations for Teachers' Work:
Professional Development Sessions

Professional development sessions at Kelly were a key organizational routine. Staff met every Friday for 90 minutes to discuss issues that were relevant to student achievement. During these meetings, an emphasis was placed on connecting teachers' instructional practices to student outcomes. While teachers often led these meetings, Dr. Johnson and other administrators also played prominent roles. In the example that follows, the principal emphasized the link between test score results, teachers' practices, and the day's professional development activity, which was focused on higher order thinking in mathematics. Dr. Johnson emphasized that Kelly students struggled with higher order thinking on the exams and that the professional development presentation would help teachers modify their teaching practices to address this issue.

Dr. Johnson stressed the importance to the teachers of "evaluating these analyses" (referring to the student-level test data showing patterns of correct and incorrect responses). "You [teachers] must refer to these" (waving the analysis she had in her hand). "In looking at these analyses," Johnson said, "our children do well in the computation part but not as well in reasoning and higher order thinking." She went on to say how it is well known that many older children, particularly in high school, perform well below the level where they should be. She said, "If our children aren't doing well in high school, it's our fault because they weren't taught in elementary school . . . something is wrong and a lot of that falls on us." She then introduced [the presenter] who she stated is "going to show us how to develop the questions for higher order thinking skills."

In professional development meetings and other settings, Dr. Johnson repeatedly argued that students' challenges could be addressed through teachers' instructional practices. She was very direct, stating that "it's our fault" if the students do not perform well in high school. She continually drilled this message home to teachers. In addition, she (along with other school leaders) provided professional development opportunities that supported teachers in their instructional improvement efforts. Often, teachers with particular expertise on important issues led these meetings. School leaders argued that these strategies were associated with the high level of responsibility that many teachers at this school held for student learning.

High Expectations for Teachers' Work: The Skill Chart

High expectations for teachers are emphasized at Kelly School. Teachers are held accountable for what students learn and are expected to continuously refine their skills through professional development. They are also expected to work hard and to demonstrate a commitment to students' success. One mechanism for ensuring that teachers remain accountable for what students learn was a skill chart developed by the assistant principal, Ms. Brown, in collaboration with teachers. While Ms. Brown spearheaded the development of the skill chart, she collaborated with teachers on its design. She came up with the initial design, shared it with teachers to get their feedback, and then refined it. The chart is a tool that contains the thinking and input of multiple organizational actors. This chart contains a template on which teachers aligned their daily lesson plans to the material tested on standardized exams, standards, and students' skill mastery. Teachers used this tool to plan instruction, and school leaders (most often the principal and assistant principal) used it to monitor instruction and what students learned. Ms. Brown described the skill chart as follows:

> [It's] an organizational tool. You look at this chart and you see that child didn't master that skill. That is something you can do in a small group. You can assign your [teacher's] aide to work with that

particular child on that skill and retest, 'cause we believe right away if the child didn't master it . . . most kids only miss it . . . by a little bit, quickly review, go over it again and retest. The child masters it, then move him on.

The use of the skill charts and the active monitoring of them by school leaders helped place the responsibility for student learning on teachers. Teachers were held accountable for all students in their classes mastering those skills that students were supposed to learn and on which they ultimately would be tested. Dr. Johnson and Ms. Brown reviewed these charts regularly. The charts gave the principal and assistant principal a "window" into the classroom and a sense of what the students were learning and how well the teacher was teaching. The leadership was stretched over the principal and assistant principal. Ms. Brown, a former teacher with significant classroom experience, developed this tool based on that experience and the expertise of current classroom teachers. Dr. Johnson, who has substantial administrative experience around curricular issues, used her skills and talents as well. By combining their expertise in monitoring instruction using the skill charts, they conveyed a sense that the expertise for designing and performing the instructional monitoring routine was distributed. In addition, the tool (the skill chart) functioned as a boundary object that helped school leaders construct understandings of teaching and learning in classrooms (see Amy Coldren's discussion in Chapter 2).

After reviewing the skill charts, Dr. Johnson reported her observations and concerns regarding student progress to teachers. For example, at one of the school's weekly professional development meetings, she emphasized the need for teachers to track students' skill mastery and to take responsibility if their children failed to learn the material.

> I noticed that the skill charts are not being filled out diligently enough. . . . We can't get lax on this. . . . If you have a lot of children not getting their skills, you need to reteach. If a lot of your children are not getting the material, it is not the children. It is something to do with the way you taught it. You can't teach the same way every year. It's always the children. People make excuses. But that does not hold up because we can take the same child in two different classes, and they can do well in one and have trouble in the other. But if you see students are having trouble, don't go on. It's going to be evident that the students are not getting it, so think of another way to teach it.

In conjunction with the school's assistant principal, Dr. Johnson held teachers responsible for student performance. Again, she emphasized that no excuses should be made based on students' perceived limitations. In a professional development meeting the following week, Dr. Johnson again connected students' performance to teachers' instructional practices.

> [The principal] said that someone inquired about Kelly and asked if the school has gifted students. She said that "our students are average. . . . Our instructional program is what makes the difference. . . . The only way we continue to improve is through hard work. Just because we did well last year [on the ITBS] does not mean anything. We have to continue to work hard and align our lesson plans."

In a conversation prior to this meeting, she mentioned that she felt that the teachers were becoming "complacent." Her statements in this meeting were geared toward making sure that this complacency did not continue. The use of this tool also connected to the broader vision of the school's leaders, that teachers' practices and hard work, rather than students' characteristics, are at the core of positive academic outcomes. As the principal stated in another professional development meeting, the school's success exists because "we work three times as hard as the teachers at other schools."

In part, then, leaders at Kelly built high expectations for teachers through closely monitoring student skill mastery and espousing a philosophy of teacher accountability in formal school routines. The skill chart, developed by the assistant principal and teachers, was a designed tool that was a constituting element of leadership practice. It functioned as a boundary object that provided school leaders with a window into the classroom and a starting point for conversations with teachers about instruction. Student test score data worked in a similar fashion. Teachers' sense of responsibility was reinforced also in formal organizational routines. As discussed above, the weekly professional development meetings were one important routine through which teachers' accountability and the virtues of hard work were reinforced.

High Expectations in Informal Discourse

Structuring a formal environment to ensure high expectations for students through the creation of organizational routines is important. However, many interactions among teachers are informal, happening in the hallways, between classes, after school, or in the teachers' lunchroom. These informal exchanges—the organization as lived—do not always map neatly onto the organization as designed. Dr. Johnson and many members of her staff were cognizant of the subtle messages that teachers sent to students and to one another during these exchanges. Because of this, Dr. Johnson attempted to monitor teachers' informal interactions to ensure that teachers' high expectations for students' learning were reinforced in the school's informal contexts. It is important to push for high expectations for students and to expect teachers to take responsibility for what students learn, but in order to support and sustain this vision, leaders must monitor the subtle but powerful messages expressed in the day-to-day life of schools.

Dr. Johnson sought to make sure that the discourse about students in the school did not reflect biases based on race or social class. She worked to transform a key aspect of the situation—the language staff used to talk about student achievement. To do this, she enlisted the support of teachers to influence the school's informal discourse. She was particularly concerned about two of the school's White teachers who she felt were more likely than other teachers to exhibit such biases. The following field note details her feelings about this issue and one strategy she employed to address the problem:

> [Dr. Johnson] said that last year she heard some of the White teachers saying things about the students that she was uncomfortable with, and the Black teachers were going along with them. She called a meeting with the Black teachers to discuss this and to tell them "when these teachers talk about the children, they will talk about you when you leave the room. It is up to you to stop them from talking about these children because we need to make sure that people are not making excuses for failure." Dr. Johnson said that some of the teachers would say things like, "These parents are having too many babies, and this parent is on drugs, or this parent has this problem." But the Black teachers need to check this. I told them that you can't participate in this kind of talk. I told them this because many of them are just out of the ghetto themselves. One of the Black teachers went back to the White teachers and told them. There is a Judas in every group. And I noticed some of the White teachers in the halls they would look at me like they were upset with me, and I didn't care because this is what I had to do."

Dr. Johnson tried to influence the informal discourse in the school by appealing to the African American teachers. The task of shaping the school's informal discourse was stretched over the principal and some of the Black teachers. In an informal interview, Dr. Johnson shared the following comments:

> Dr. Johnson then began to talk about one of the teachers (Mr. J.). She said that she feels he has a problem with Black boys. She said that one day they were taking up a collection for the United Negro College Fund and that Mr. J. . . . said, "I make my donation by coming here everyday" [implying that his donation is working at this school]. She

responded by saying, "You get a pay check every time you come into this school. This is not charity." This is an example, she argued, of the attitudes that some White teachers have. . . . Dr. Johnson said that she sees a lot of behaviors in [Mr. J.] that suggest that he can't get along with Black boys. And that he does not like children. . . . She says, "He does not know how to talk to them. Children know when you like them, and he does not seem to like them." She added, "I have to keep an eye on him because I do not trust him."

Dr. Johnson's concerns about Mr. J. in particular appear to be well founded. In the teachers' lounge a few weeks later, Mr. J. was engaged in a conversation about student performance and connected it to the lack of parents' commitment and support.

> Several of the teachers came in with their lunches to eat and talk to one another. Mr. J said that if the students are getting a "D" that should be the parents' grade. He said that the student's report card is a reflection of the parents. If the students are doing poorly, if they are getting "Ds" and "Fs," then the parents are messing up, at least most of the time.

Mr. J. went on to question how he could effectively teach without the support of parents. While no one challenged his statement directly, a biracial (White/African American) Spanish teacher raised issues related to the struggles that some parents face in difficult neighborhoods that can inhibit their ability to support school-based education. The Spanish teacher's comments changed the tone of the conversation. As the conversation continued, Mr. J. seemed to acknowledge these challenges and place less direct blame on parents.

One of the key characteristics of teacher responsibility for student learning is that teachers do not blame parents for challenges associated with students' outcomes. While Mr. J. attached blame for students' failure squarely on the shoulders of their parents, the Spanish teacher sought to move the conversation away from the parents themselves to other circumstances that might impact their involvement. This represented the kind of shift in informal discourse that the principal sought. It also showed how a teacher with no formal leadership designation (the Spanish teacher) took responsibility for leadership by seeking to impact teachers' perceptions of parents and, by association, students. Leadership (in this case the shifting of the school discourse about students and parents) was stretched across both formally designated and informal leaders—the principal and this teacher.

Dr. Johnson's efforts did seem to influence the overall tenor of conversations at the school. While much of the discourse about students in many low-income, African American schools focuses on students' deficits and reflects a reduced sense of teachers' responsibility for students' outcomes (Diamond et al., 2004), conversations among Kelly's staff were often very positive with respect to students. The following exchange is illustrative:

> I spent time in the lunchroom today after an interview with Ms. Grant [the school's fifth-grade teacher]. In the time I spent, there was not a whole lot discussed. A few things about the students came up. . . . [The seventh-grade teacher] was reading some of the work of her students. They were supposed to discuss what things are going to be like in the year 2005. Would it be better or worse? One child had written something somewhat impressive, and [the teacher] said [in a complementary tone], "Look at Kiana trying to write." She then showed the work to [the sixth-grade teacher], and she acted very impressed.

Praising students for their academic work in a public setting like the teachers' lounge is in line with the principal's desire to influence teachers' informal discourse about students, even though it is not clear that the teachers' comments in this case resulted from the principal's efforts. Other teachers also expressed the belief that students were capable of achieving at high levels. For example, Ms. Grant expressed concern that she was not challenging some of her students enough. Following a meeting with a high-achieving student's parents during parent–teacher conferences, she said:

> I get concerned because I don't want her to just be sitting here taking the year off because she knows everything already. So I have started going beyond the advanced work in my book to try and push the students, and she still always knows the answer. Some of the other students know most of the answers, but this child always knows. I can count on her (she puts her hand up in the air imitating the girl). So I plan to go on the Internet when I get home to search for other work for them to do.

The challenge articulated by Ms. Grant was to make sure that the students in her class were engaged and pushed appropriately by the material. Her expectations for her students were high and she sought to push them to achieve academically by adjusting her instructional practices.

Finally, an exchange among grades 3–8 teachers at a grade-level meeting, a key organizational routine at Kelly, later in the school year also demonstrated the teachers' recognizing the students' talents.

A second teacher said that during one of her classes she was sitting next to a child. "He almost made me crack up in the classroom because I wasn't expecting it. He started singing 'Billy Jean is not my lover,'" (singing the Michael Jackson song) "and then said, 'Michael Jackson is not my brother.' I had to leave the room because he cracked me up." Ms. Grant then said, "He is funny." Another teacher said that one of his students wrote on his assignment that he had learned about the sax player Jason Carter, writing, "I learned about a great sax player named Jason Carter today. I have an uncle named Jason Carter. I wonder if they are related." He then laughed along with the rest of the teachers.

This teacher continued, saying that another little girl wrote on her assignment, "I learned a lot about music and writing songs today. I also learned that the other students in the class can't sing." He laughed and the other teachers laughed with him (I laughed too).

Ms. Grant, who was several months pregnant, said that one of her male students said, "All she does in the classroom is eat and rub her stomach." Ms. Grant demonstrated how he imitated her and then he said that she digs in her mouth and eats the leftover food. This was all said in a joking tone with admiration for the boy's storytelling ability and sense of humor. Again, the other teachers in the room laughed when the story was told.

While these exchanges do not relate directly to students' academic capacity, they do demonstrate that teachers' discourse about students at the school was not entirely negative. The culture of the school left room for the appreciation of students as well as criticism of them. I argue that this was at least in part a reflection of the emphasis placed on high expectations for students in school leadership and management practice. These expectations were cultivated, I argue, in the interactions of school leaders, teachers, and aspects of the situation such as tools and discourses that reinforced high expectations for students and a sense of students' capabilities for achievement. This situation—routines, tools, language—was built through leadership practice.

High Expectations Among Students

In addition to building high expectations among the teachers, school leaders believed that students needed to see themselves as capable. To do this, an effort was made to highlight African American history, culture, and accomplishments through a set of cultural relevance organizational routines that involved students and teachers. Every day at Kelly, school began with the traditional national anthem and the Black national anthem "Lift Every Voice and

Sing." These anthems were followed by a Black history fact and the recitation of the Kelly school pledge, which reinforced that students would work hard and achieve. The school also celebrated the students' African American heritage with hallway decorations that included pictures of African American celebrities and historical figures and representative students' projects, including African masks and African history exhibits. The school also hosted a Kwanzaa celebration annually, in which the entire school community (including hundreds of parents) participated. As the principal explained:

> We teach them about their heritage from the moment they step in the building, which is evident with our morning opening, and when we do the national anthem, we also do the black national anthem, "Lift Every Voice," and we have a "thought for today," and we also have a quiz daily, a trivial kind of question based upon Black history.

In the creation of a school vision that supported high expectations for students, each of the cultural relevance routines was essential for addressing this function. Each routine illustrated the distribution of leadership. First, leadership was *stretched over* leaders and tools. The pictures on the wall, the samples of student work, and the singing of the Black national anthem were all constitutive of leadership practice—leadership was stretched over these tools and intentionally connected to selling the vision of students' capabilities. Second, creating this environment also reflected a set of interactions among multiple formal and informal leaders. Teachers worked together to coordinate class assignments that would build a thematic emphasis on students' African American heritage, while student work was collected and posted by teachers. Multiple teachers also were instrumental in leading the preparation for the Kwanzaa celebration. Each classroom performed as part of the celebration, and some teachers, particularly the second- and fourth-grade teachers, played leadership roles in organizing the program. The fourth-grade teacher worked with a small group of other teachers to organize the logistical arrangements (e.g., planning a menu and ordering food), while the second-grade teacher, who has a musical theatre background, worked with students to develop their vocal skills in preparation for the event. Even if mundane, these activities were interdependent—they helped to support the cultivation of a positive, affirming environment for Black students and reinforced the belief that they were capable learners with a proud heritage.

While many schools use some of these strategies, Kelly's leaders connected these practices to their overall vision for educational improvement. Dr. Johnson connected this knowledge of African American history to students' confidence and achievement. She stated, "I want them to be confident. And that's the reason why we have the Black history. Because I believe if you don't know your history, then somebody else will tell you the history they want you to know."

LEARNING THE KELLY PHILOSOPHY:
THE INDUCTION OF MS. GRANT

While it is clear from the preceding discussion that teachers' sense of responsibility for student learning was a key focus of leadership practice at Kelly, whether and how leadership and classroom practice connected is another matter. Indeed much work on school leadership skips straight over classroom instruction in efforts to detect a relationship between school leadership arrangements on the one hand and student achievement on the other. While student achievement is the bottom line, a critical issue concerns how school leadership and management practice works through classroom practice to improve student learning. To explore this connection, I discuss how Ms. Grant, a first-year, fifth-grade teacher, was introduced to Kelly School. In particular, I focus on her relationship with her mentor teacher. Through being inducted into schools, new teachers are exposed to the way things are done in the new setting and receive many cues about what is and is not expected of them. Thus, the teacher induction process provides an excellent opportunity to learn about a school's culture and how it is communicated to teachers. In this section, I focus on the messages that Ms. Grant understood from her interactions with other teachers and administrators, and on how her classroom practices were connected with leadership practice at Kelly, especially the push for high expectations for students and sense of responsibility for student learning among teachers.

Ms. Grant came to Kelly School from a corporate job in the city. She was in her late 20s and was expecting her second child. When the research began, she had been in the school for only about 1 month. She described her adjustment to the school as smooth largely because of the support of the administration (i.e., principal and assistant principal) and her mentor teacher, Ms. Whitten, who was an experienced upper-grade-level special education teacher. In discussing her relationship with Ms. Whitten, Ms. Grant explained that she was "right there . . . by my side . . . helping me out with a lot of stuff that I had questions about." According to Ms. Grant, this "stuff" included administrative issues such as organizing her grade book and the legalities of attendance policies, as well as issues related more directly to instruction. Ms. Whitten was also fond of Ms. Grant, whom she described as "an excellent person to work with and mentor. Anything that I advised her to do, she did."

In communicating with Ms. Grant, Ms. Whitten emphasized the connection between student learning and teaching practices. She encouraged Ms. Grant to be well prepared for every class and to tailor her teaching practices to students' needs. With regard to preparation, Ms. Grant recounts that Ms. Whitten told her, "You should have your day planned, be ready." Ms. Grant said, "And that came easily because I would literally be panicked about it the night before. So when I come in, in the morning, I've already got an idea based upon what we'd done yesterday what we should be doing today."

In line with the school's overall discourse, Ms. Grant communicated high expectations for her students. While she argued that some of the students were lazy at the beginning of the school year, she felt that they were all capable of doing well. She communicated her high expectations to her students as a means of encouraging their performance. As she explained during an interview, "I told them that Thursday. You know, I sat down and I go, 'You guys, man, I can see three quarters of you all making honor roll.' I really, really could, and that's a good feeling." During classroom instruction, Ms. Grant encouraged students to reach their full potential, often pushing students who struggled to keep trying.

Early in the year, Ms. Grant expressed frustration regarding her students' performance on exams. As she explained, "Too many of the students weren't testing well. Too many of the students weren't scoring high enough. When I know that they're smart. Too many of them were getting problems wrong that they shouldn't be getting wrong." Ms. Grant shared her frustration about students' outcomes with Ms. Whitten, who emphasized adjustments to her instructional practices. Ms. Whitten explained:

> [Ms. Grant] came to me, and she said, "I'm teaching a skill, but the kids just aren't getting it." I said, "Reteach it." I said, "They're not gonna get it." I said, because this was in the very beginning. And she said, "I taught this skill and I tested them on Friday like you told me." She said, "And you know they didn't get it." I said, "Well then you reteach it." I said, "What you do," I said, "on Monday reteach the skill, reintroduce the skill." I said, "You go over practice problems with them on the board." I said, "Children need visuals. . . . You either use the blackboard or the overhead projector, whichever one you feel comfortable with." . . . On Tuesday, I said, "You give them a few problems on Monday to go home to practice on. On Tuesday when they come back, you go over those problems with them on the board. So everyone can see, everyone will know. You know what mistakes they made." I said, "Then you reteach the skill on Tuesday. You go over it again. On Wednesday, you practice." . . . You know they're practicing, they practice Tuesday night, they practice on

Wednesday. . . . By Thursday they should know the skill, and you go over the practice with them. I said, "Taking papers home and grading them yourself is not gonna help the student. Because he doesn't know what he did incorrectly."

In this exchange the mentor teacher emphasized the teacher's responsibility for ensuring that the students learned the material. Ms. Grant believed that the students were capable, stating, "I know that they're smart." However, Ms. Whitten tied students' struggles directly to Ms. Grant's instructional practices, recommending that she adjust how she was teaching the material. She communicated the critical role of Ms. Grant's instruction in shaping student learning and emphasized that students will learn the material if given the opportunity. In a similar vein, Ms. Whitten encouraged Ms. Grant to use homework as a learning opportunity rather than simply for evaluation. The overall message to Ms. Grant was that she was responsible for her students' learning and that the students were capable of learning the material.

As Ms. Whitten had indicated, Ms. Grant's reports of her instructional practices and my observations demonstrated an acceptance of Ms. Whitten's recommendations.

> *Ms. Grant (MG):* They just needed more time. You gotta adjust accordingly when they need a little bit more review. It doesn't mean they don't get it, just means they need a little bit more refresher time that's all.
>
> *JD:* And were there um, when you realized it, what did you do?
>
> *MG:* I spread it out.
>
> *JD:* OK?
>
> *MG:* For instance, I'll review long division. If I start on Monday and I see if I give like a quiz on Wednesday and they're not doing well, then I'll, I take extra time. I'll steal some time from another subject or I'll push the quiz for Friday to Monday and a lot more time for them to get it. I'll have more students at the board, some at my desk. You know, I'll have to . . . I'll have to throw out all the chips. I have to implement more stuff so this starts clicking to them again. I'll be at the board, I'll put them in groups. . . . But I'll, in essence, I'll give them 2 or 3 more days to catch up. Because, you know, it's all stacked on top of each other.
>
> *JD:* Right.
>
> *MG:* There's no sense in me leaving three-digit by three-digit multiplication to go to division if they ain't getting three-digit by three-digit. Just drilling them, just gotta keep drilling them. And then they get it.

> *JD:* OK. But there's a point at which they, it clicks?
>
> *MG:* Um-hmm, it does.
>
> *JD:* So you use repetition a lot?
>
> *MG:* Absolutely. Give it to them like bell ringers. I just keep giving it to them, just keep giving it to them until it starts, till the steps click, click in. Kind of carry it on. Oh that's right, 6 times 8 is 48 because we did a problem yesterday. I mean you know, blah, blah, blah, after awhile it becomes second nature.

Ms. Grant clearly sees her students as capable learners. She also sees herself as responsible for giving them adequate opportunities to learn the material she teaches. As a new teacher, she received this message through the induction process, particularly from her mentor teacher.

While much of the relationship between Ms. Grant and Ms. Whitten is one on one, Ms. Whitten also talks with Ms. Brown and Dr. Johnson about Ms. Grant's progress. Ms. Whitten says of the principal and assistant principal:

> [They] call me in from time to time and ask me how she was doing. And I would tell [them] she's doing great. . . . Of course, she doesn't have the skill and expertise that a person that was trained in education would have. But she had the discipline and was a very hard worker and a very intelligent woman. So I told Dr. Johnson, I said, "She's doing what she needs to do." You know and she will get the techniques down.

As we can see from this passage, leadership for instruction in this school was socially distributed. The mentor teacher provided direct assistance to Ms. Grant but communicated how she was performing to administrators. Leadership for instruction was "stretched across" the mentor teacher and the administrators. This arrangement created leadership that would not be possible if any one person worked alone.

CONCLUSION

In this chapter, I have used Kelly Elementary School, a high-performing Chicago Public School, to examine leadership practice from a distributed perspective. In particular, I have focused on how school leaders used several organizational routines in an effort to raise expectations for students among teachers and to increase teachers' sense of responsibility for student learning. First, school leaders and teachers devoted 90 minutes each week to discussing substantive educational issues. Through these meetings, a formal discourse was created that emphasized students' capacity for high achievement and the link between teachers' practices and student outcomes. Second, school leaders developed and utilized the skill chart, a document that served as a tool for connecting teachers' lesson plans to standards, testing, and students' skill mastery. The use of the skill charts reinforced the message about students' capacity and teachers' responsibility. The cultivation of these beliefs involved multiple leaders working together with tools and routines. In addition to the formal discourse, school leaders sought to influence the informal, day-to-day, school discourse to emphasize students' positive attributes and abilities. They did this by enlisting teachers to shape informal conversations.

Third, school leaders encouraged high academic achievement through a set of cultural relevance organizational routines that emphasized students' accomplishments and sought to reinforce students' beliefs in their own potential. The playing of the Black National Anthem, prominent displays of selected students' work, and displays and activities that sought to honor students' cultural heritage all contributed to an organizational environment geared toward facilitating academic achievement among students.

Finally, I used the case of Ms. Grant, a new teacher being introduced to Kelly School, to explore how school leadership practice connected with a new teacher and with her classroom practices. Ms. Grant's introduction to the school provides an excellent example of the social distribution of leadership. Ms. Whitten, Ms. Grant's mentor teacher, was the conduit through which the school's vision was communicated to Ms. Grant. Ms. Whitten's advice for Ms. Grant was in line with the overall message of the school's leaders—high expectations for students and a high degree of responsibility for student performance on the part of teachers. The ongoing communication between Ms. Whitten and the administration provided a window into Ms. Grant's classroom that did not require the presence of the principal or the assistant principal. It also allowed the core messages of school leaders to be conveyed to Ms. Grant.

5

The Leadership Struggle: The Case of Costen Elementary School

Tim Hallett
INDIANA UNIVERSITY

A long-time principal, beloved by the faculty, retires and is replaced by an administration that, for the most part, maintains the status quo. Then a new principal is hired with an external mandate for change, only to be met with hostility by the faculty while discourse about instruction and its improvement comes to a halt. This scenario casts light on the trials and tribulations of Mrs. Kox as the new principal at Costen Elementary School.

Despite the growing literature that places the principal at the center of instructional leadership (Hallinger & Heck, 1996a, 1996b, 1998; Prestine & Nelson, 2005), the story of Costen Elementary reminds us that leadership does not lie dormant inside of official positions. This point is implicit in the literature on principal succession (Ball, 1987; Miskel & Cosgrove, 1985). Ironically, the infusion of new administrative personnel can promote old inertia instead of transformative directions as people cling passionately to the established practices with which they are familiar (Gouldner, 1954). The challenges of succession illustrate some of the hidden tensions of leadership, and these tensions gain additional clarity when we take a distributed perspective (Gronn, 2002; Spillane et al., 2004): Leadership involves a living, breathing relationship among leaders, followers, and an evolving situation. These relationships do not exist a priori. They have to be created, and it is often a *struggle* to establish them.

The case of Costen Elementary School tells us about what I call the "leadership struggle," the hidden, often-ugly relational "underside" of leadership that is glossed over by a myopic focus on success. This struggle can be a painful one, and the story of this struggle at Costen School has four interrelated parts. It is a story about a new principal's struggle to develop a relationship with the teachers in order to create and forge a new leadership practice. It is a struggle in the era of high-stakes accountability where the principal is caught between district office demands and keeping her staff, the very people on whom she depends to meet those demands, happy. It is the struggle of a principal intent on cracking the cellular classroom structure that characterizes so many schools in an effort to create a structure where classroom practices are deprivatized and more standardized. And, it is the story of the teachers' response.

To tell this story, I draw on 2 years of ethnographic study inside Costen School. I start by introducing Mrs. Kox, and then I describe how she grappled with the context of the school, a contradictory situation characterized by the new era of accountability and old norms of teacher autonomy. Next, I examine how Mrs. Kox tried to shape this context by emphasizing accountability. Finally, I describe the teachers' response and how the contentious relations at Costen affected instructional discourse.

MRS. KOX'S PERSONAL STYLE

Perhaps the only thing more daunting than a kindergartener's first day at school is a new principal's first day on the job. However, Mrs. Kox is an intrepid soul and a strong woman, and she dove into her new job with passion and conviction. She knew that change could be hard, and that some of her efforts would anger incumbent teachers, but she advocated, "If you're willing to take the position, that [anger] comes with the job. It just comes with the job." She was not afraid of making hard decisions, even in the face of resistance, because as she said, "If I know I'm right, I'm not giving in." Mrs. Kox recalled how she learned from one of her mentors: "I worked under a new principal when I first became an assistant principal, and she has gotten a lot of resistance, and I saw how she handled them [teachers]. And she is a very strong person, and she never backed down." As she reiterated to me many times, "My role is not to be popular. It is to get things done." Mrs. Kox was determined to stand on her principles, and she refused to pander to different groups. In her own words, she "doesn't play games" and she is "like a rock."

Mrs. Kox's principles were shaped by her experiences in principal leadership training in education (PLTE), a highly selective and prestigious administrative training program. PLTE is a joint venture between an elite business school and an elite school of education, and it is believed to represent the best in leadership training. As a fellow at PLTE, Mrs. Kox encountered the most recent thinking on school leadership: The principal is an instructional leader who is responsible for setting a vision for instruction and monitoring its practice in the classroom. In good schools, instruction is not a private classroom affair but a public practice that is accessible and open to all.

Mrs. Kox also was shaped by PLTE's business principles. She was impressed by this aspect because "in education, if we don't cross over and learn from the business field, we won't have the effectiveness because business-people have a different orientation to improvement. They have a better sense of urgency." Kox's business-like sense of urgency and focus on the bottom line also happened to fit the educational policy trend in Chicago that emphasized accountability for student improvement.

Mrs. Kox said that she learned about two types of leaders at PLTE: "The leader who has a lot of structure, [and] a 'symbolic someone' who is articulate and has a good P.R. personality." Kox identified with the former and told me, "I don't seek to be popular. I don't seek to be well liked. Hopefully it's a good management style that can move people forward."

These very traits resonated strongly with the Local School Council (LSC)[1] as it went through the process of hiring a new principal. The chair of the LSC, Stan Feierman, described how they had interviewed almost two dozen candidates, but "Mrs. Kox was far and away the best as far as I was personally concerned." Mr. Feierman elaborated:

> She had been through PLTE, number one. She was very articulate. She was obviously very committed. . . . I think that the job of principal . . . is much more demanding now than it was 10 years ago when I first started doing this. The dictates that come from the Board of Ed are much more severe, the whole issue of testing being the one and only thing that matters, accountability is very tight all the way around. The only person in the school who's really responsible is the principal, and we needed to know we had someone who could really take the lead.

Based on her training and the pressures of accountability, Mr. Feierman thought Mrs. Kox was the person to "take the lead" because "she's very opinionated and has very high standards" and "she seemed very tenacious, she seemed very intelligent, very well spoken and I guess—she had a lot of energy and a lot of integrity as far as I was concerned." When I asked Jessica Churley (the LSC secretary) what made Mrs. Kox a good candidate, she commented on Mrs. Kox and her assistant principal, Mrs. Milbern: "I think they're very tough. I think they're very no-nonsense. They're not afraid of confrontation."

These are some of the reasons why the LSC felt that Mrs. Kox was an ideal candidate to lead the school through the myriad new accountability policies that were creating unprecedented pressures for school change. This leads us to a discussion of the school context that confronted Mrs. Kox when she arrived at Costen Elementary.

GETTING STARTED: COMING TO TERMS
WITH THE PRIOR SCHOOL ORDER
IN THE NEW ERA OF ACCOUNTABILITY

We had a principal [Mr. Welch], he's a really good guy and what he did was he hired good people who he let do their jobs. And his assistant principal was a strong woman but she was the same way, she let people do their jobs.

The old administration was more of a delegating authority. Where she [Jackson] was the head person and she would allow the teacher to do whatever it is they want.

The distributed leadership perspective forces us to recognize that leadership is not simply about people, but also about the situation, and when Mrs. Kox arrived at Costen School she inherited organizational arrangements—routines, culture, norms—that the teachers and the prior administrations had developed over time. The teachers had been left alone to "do their jobs" without the burden of outside intervention. They were free to "do whatever it is they want" in the classroom. These organizational arrangements had been in place for over 10 years and across two previous administrations, the first led by Mr. Welch, the next by Mrs. Jackson.

During Mr. Welch's tenure the teachers and the administration had negotiated a system of high classroom autonomy and low administrative surveillance. Indeed, Costen resembled the classic description of many American schools (Bidwell, 1965; Lortie, 1975). This arrangement placed great confidence in the skills of Costen's veteran teaching staff and provided them with substantial flexibility in their efforts to meet the diverse needs of the students, resembling what Rosenholtz (1989a) termed a "non-routine technical culture." A teacher explained:

The first administration—when I first started in 1991—was a man [Welch] who was very, very laid back, and we have a lot of creative teachers in this school and you pretty much were able to do what you needed to do and use your creativity and kind of go with your own flow more or less.

The classroom was the individual teacher's domain, and the teachers closed their doors and did their own thing without interference from school administrators. Instruction was mostly a private matter between teacher and students. Early in my fieldwork, I was able to observe the legacy of this autonomy-based order. Many teachers relied on a skill-centered, teacher-driven pedagogy, while some used a more constructivist, open-ended, inquiry-based pedagogy. Some teachers taught reading through phonics, while others taught whole language. Some used textbooks, while others used trade books. In math, some teachers used an innovative curriculum that featured hands-on manipulatives, while others used traditional direct instruction techniques. The teachers also had their own styles of classroom management. Some were rigid authoritarians, while others developed sophisticated reward systems to promote good behavior.

During the Welch era, one of the important roles of the principal was to buffer teachers from the interference of district policies and other external pressures. This became increasingly difficult with the emergence of state- and citywide standards late in Mr. Welch's tenure. Standardization threatened the norm of teacher autonomy, but Mr. Welch resisted these policies and maintained a loose coupling between the reforms and the teachers' individualized practices (Meyer & Rowan, 1977, 1978). In particular, Mr. Welch resisted the purview of the LSC and the accountability that it had come to represent. For example, during an LSC meeting, the former chair, who worked with Mr. Welch, told Mrs. Kox:

> [Mr. Welch] would bring me documents and would say, "Sign this." And, uh, he just wanted my signature because it was the law. But, you know, he wouldn't give me the opportunity to examine what I was signing, and he didn't want the council to know.

Likewise, Mr. Feierman said that that during Mr. Welch's tenure, "curriculum issues were never the purview, were never allowed to be the purview of the LSC. In fact, I was actively discouraged."

The staff loved Mr. Welch and his laissez-faire style, and when he retired, the long-time assistant principal took his place for 1 year before retiring. For the most part, the next principal, Mrs. Jackson, kept this arrangement intact. In a nod toward standardization, Mrs. Jackson used the school's discretionary funds to hire a consulting firm to align the school's curriculum with state and city standards. However, this act was largely ceremonial (Meyer & Rowan, 1977), as the teachers held onto their own autonomous classroom practices. One teacher described the new curriculum by saying:

> Everyone kind of realized that this is something that's not going to be used. Something that we're doing because [Mrs. Jackson] wants us to do it. . . . It was something unnecessary. I think that's why a lot of people don't use it.

Mrs. Jackson did not force the new curriculum onto the teachers, and the teachers told me that it sat dormant on their shelves, or that they drew from it selectively. The teachers' autonomy increased when Mrs. Jackson left the school at the start of the 1998–99 school year to take a position with the consulting firm that had aligned Costen's curriculum. A teacher explained, "We really were running ourselves before Mrs. Kox got here. In fact, school started without a principal, and we did very well."

This was the established order that Mrs. Kox inherited when she started at the school in January 1999. However, this inheritance was somewhat unwitting because Mrs. Kox had little sense of how the school had been operating when she arrived at Costen. Her lack of knowledge was exacerbated by the fact that the established order existed only in the minds and practices of the staff: When Mrs. Kox began work there was no documentation of the school's operation.[2] During my first day of fieldwork, Kox told me, "We're fine tuning a lot of procedures. When I came in, the old administration didn't leave anything, so we're really starting from the bottom." When she arrived at the school, the principal's office was barren, and she explained, "It's hard when there's a history of things that are done, and you don't know anything about it." Some of the teachers and Stan Feierman corroborated the story.

> The fact is that Denise [Kox] came into a school where there were no records, where there was no structure, and she had to create it. From scratch. Which she should not have had to do. You know, there should have been something she could take over. . . . She was actually trying to bring order to a disordered situation.

In one sense, Mr. Feierman is correct. It is not easy to take over an organization with no documentation. However, when he says that there was "no structure," he is incorrect. There *was* a structure at the school. The school *did* have an order, but Mrs. Kox could not learn about it from written documents.[3]

Although Mrs. Kox did not know about the established norm of autonomy and the teachers' individualized routines, she *did know* that accountability policies and pressures had been steadily increasing since the mid-1990s.

These policies emanated from both the state and the city. At the statewide level, some basic curriculum, instructional, and testing standards had been developed as a way to create uniformity so that schools could be usefully compared with one another. These comparisons created an additional wave of accountability reforms in Chicago because of the dismal performance of Chicago schools on standardized tests. From 1988–1995, the Chicago Public Schools had been experimenting with a school-based governance approach that emphasized LSCs. Under this plan, schools and their LSCs were given broad autonomy to formulate their own improvement plans. When this approach did not yield gains in test scores, the Mayor of Chicago, in 1995, went in the opposite direction of centralized control. He oversaw further standardization of the curriculum across the city, and he established rigid benchmarks for student promotion based on standardized test scores. He also appointed a "Chief Executive Officer" of city schools and gave the CEO the rational-legal authority to place low-scoring schools on probation. If these schools did not show improvement on standardized tests, the CEO could have them closed and reconstituted. However, the CEO's ability to reward and punish schools created pressure to improve test scores across the system, and not just for the schools that were facing probation. The era of high-stakes accountability had begun. With this shift in policy, LSCs were placed under the umbrella of accountability. As some of the quotes cited earlier suggest, this was the policy backdrop for the LSC's decision to hire Mrs. Kox.

Because of their position as middle managers (Spillane et al., 2002), principals have the double strain of implementing the policies within their schools while facing accountability themselves. Accountability policies put enormous pressure on Mrs. Kox to act in ways that would improve the school. As an assistant principal explained:

> The principal goes down for a rating with the REO [Regional Education Officer]. And the first question the REO is going to say to the principal is: "How'd you do with reading and math?" It's measurable. It's empirical data. It's something you can hold somebody accountable for. I'm not saying it's the end all, but it is. Secondly, "How's your attendance rate? What were your statistics on your [student] misconduct? Your [student] behavior?"

Mrs. Kox's standing with the regional office depended in part on the school's measurable improvement, but accountability also fit Mrs. Kox's personal beliefs. As she told me, "I had heard this phrase so much when I was teaching, 'You can't reach every child. If you can reach at least 80% of them, you are successful.' That's just not a standard I can live with." Mrs. Kox passionately believed in high standards and continued improvement.

To summarize, Mrs. Kox entered a situation that was characterized by an established system of teacher autonomy, as well as new pressures for standardization and accountability. This contradictory context and the commitment of different people to the poles of autonomy and accountability lead us to a key element of the situation: the school's standardized test scores and the various interpretations of them.

When Mrs. Kox arrived at the school in 1999, 55.7% of the students at Costen were scoring at or above national norms in reading on the Iowa Test of Basic Skills, while 57.9% of students did so in math. When viewed through the lens of accountability and high achievement, these marks are not spectacular, and Mrs. Kox saw considerable room for improvement: "When I look at the test results, 50% are succeeding. I look at it the other way. Fifty percent of our children are not succeeding. . . . Bottom line is the kids have to bring those grades up to apply for the best high schools." Indeed, it is the tragedy of urban education that some people would deem as acceptable a situation in which nearly half of the students were not performing at grade level. This standard would never be accepted in the wealthy White suburbs that surround Chicago, and 3 years before accountability policies were signed into *federal* law, Mrs. Kox was determined to leave no child behind.

However, Costen's ITBS scores were much better than the citywide average. In 1999, the citywide average was a miserable 39.1% for reading and 43.4% for math. Ironically, the very metric created by accountability made Costen look comparatively good, and the situation that Mrs. Kox viewed as unacceptable was interpreted differently by the veteran teachers at Costen. In their view, they were doing an extraordinary job under difficult circumstances. Costen is a big school that is burdened by large classroom sizes and an enrollment approaching 1,500 students. The school serves multiple immigrant groups, and Costen has bilingual programs in Spanish, Russian, and Urdu.[4] Numerous other students receive English as a second language instruction (ESL), and overall more than 40% of the students are classified as "limited English." The mobility rate[5] is over 30%, and from 1990–1998 the percentage of low-income students increased from 44% to 73%. Despite these challenges, Costen had its share of success. Of the 10 largest public elementary schools in the city, Costen's ITBS scores were among the very best. Moreover, the school's reading scores had been on a steady *increase,* up 14 percentage points since 1991 (although math scores were stable).

Given Costen's relative success, the teachers resisted Mrs. Kox's efforts to frame the situation at the school as a problematic one in need of improvement (Coburn, 2005; Spillane et al., 2002). For example, during a faculty meeting early in my fieldwork, Mrs. Kox tried to frame the situation as in need of change by saying, "Costen is a good school. The former administration did a good job, but we can't take it for granted. Society is changing." She continued, "We are putting those preventative resources in place. Why should we wait for a disaster?" Then she told the teachers, "You've got to have higher expectations, because [the students] are going to be taking care of you someday." However, a teacher quickly interjected, "But our scores are going up." Mrs. Kox responded, "But our students are changing, and we want to ensure that *everyone* is going up." Mrs. Kox framed the school's changing demographics as a motivation to get better. But then another teacher responded with a different interpretation: "We're getting more and more kids now with problems at home. There's no discipline in the household, and I can model things here, but if they don't get it at home . . ." When Mrs. Kox tried to make the case for improvement, the first teacher rejected Mrs. Kox's definition of the problem, and the second teacher rejected Kox's belief that classroom changes could generate higher student achievement.

At another meeting, Mrs. Kox turned the floor over to Mrs. D. (an upper-grade literacy teacher) so she could share with colleagues what she had learned at an off-campus staff development meeting where the city introduced its new "structured curriculum." Mrs. D. told her colleagues, "First of all, people were really angry at the meeting because [the city] spent so much materials on this," when it is really just a set of lesson plans that are aligned with the statewide goals. Then a teacher asked, "I thought this was just for schools on probation?" Another teacher who had been at the meeting answered, "It's not mandated except for schools that are on probation." Then Mrs. D. reiterated her negative interpretation by saying, "For those of you who have been in Chicago schools before . . . it's just like the old punch cards" and a "waste." Since Costen had relatively good test scores, it was in not in danger of being put on academic probation. As a result, many of the teachers rejected any interpretation of the situation that suggested a need to standardize their autonomous teaching practices.

The situation at Costen was characterized by rival organizational logics (Heimer, 1999; Ingersoll, 2003), and the contradictory tensions between the old autonomy and the new accountability created different interpretations of this situation. However, in Mrs. Kox's calculus, accountability won out, partly because the LSC had hired her with accountability in mind, but also because she had little working knowledge of how the school had been operating and because accountability fit with her own beliefs. Just as she said she would do in her interviews, Mrs. Kox stood firm on her convictions.

MRS. KOX'S EFFORTS TO ESTABLISH ACCOUNTABILITY-BASED LEADERSHIP PRACTICES

People are held more accountable under Kox's administration. There's more accountability of what teachers are doing now. (Teacher interview)

Mrs. Kox likes to get her hands in and say, "What's going on here?
This is what we're going to have to do," rather than just allow the
teacher to do it. (Teacher interview)

Like many new principals, Mrs. Kox was intent on improving student
achievement at her school, and to do so she used the authority of her position
to create changes that were inspired by accountability. When I asked teachers
to compare Mrs. Kox with the previous administrations, they broadly cited
"accountability" in the form of Mrs. Kox's increased surveillance of and intervention in teaching practices. More specifically, Mrs. Kox tried to crack open
the cellular classroom structure that characterizes many schools, as a way to
facilitate transparency and deprivatize the teachers' idiosyncratic practices by
creating more standardization. In what follows, I outline three of Mrs. Kox's
attempts to establish accountability-based leadership practices: her purview of
classroom and student management, grading, and curriculum and instruction.[6]

Classroom and Student Management

One of the most immediate ways that Mrs. Kox attempted to deprivatized teachers' classroom practices was by entering their classrooms. City
policy requires formal classroom observations twice a year. However, Mrs.
Kox would frequently "pop" into classrooms unannounced, often when
making her daily morning rounds. Mrs. Kox even encouraged me to do the
same thing because "without some external partner to come in and observe,
I don't think it will get us to do what we need to do." I decided not to do this
because I feared it would alienate the teachers. However, I witnessed Mrs.
Kox's unplanned visits on many occasions.

Mrs. Kox heads to room 124. She enters and stands inside the
doorway. The students are sitting quietly as the teacher is doing
something at her desk. Mrs. Kox observes for a few seconds, but does
not say anything. Then we head upstairs to room 224, and Mrs. Kox
does the same thing.

Mrs. Kox stands in the doorway of a classroom. The teacher is taking
attendance and collecting lunch money. The noise increases as the
teacher tells the students, "My name is not 1st National Bank. Please
bring, if you can, correct money, because last week the lunch lady got
quite mad at me." Then Mrs. Kox moves further in and walks around
the room. She looks over the students' shoulders to assess what
appears to be their homework (though she says nothing). The room is
quite and we leave.

> Mrs. Kox opens the door to a classroom and the students are scurrying around their desks. The noise rises, and Mrs. Kox asks the teacher, "Why are they running?" The teacher responds, "They're running to get their books." Mrs. Kox says, "That's unacceptable," and makes the students settle down, telling them, "Show me your learning position." Once the students are sitting quietly, Mrs. Kox instructs them, "Stand up, get what you need for science, and put your book bags away. You have 5 seconds. Five . . . four . . . three . . . two . . . one . . ." The students move quickly but quietly and return to their seats. Mrs. Kox tells them, "Straighten up the books around you." Then she walks around the room checking their homework and telling them, "Raise your hand before you speak." When the students settle down, Mrs. Kox says, "OK, we are ready for learning. See you at lunchtime. Have a good day."

During these visits, Kox paid particular attention to the teachers' grip on student behavior. She preferred quite, calm classrooms, and she would intervene if she felt necessary.

While this practice fit the logic of accountability, it disrupted the classroom autonomy of the past. In comparing Mrs. Kox with the previous administrations, one teacher invoked the imagery of "Big Brother." He described how Mrs. Kox is "more visible in the building," and how the teachers see her "in the cafeteria," and "in the halls, popping out of lockers, popping out of closets." Indeed, Kox held the teachers accountable not only for student behavior inside the classroom, but outside as well. Whenever Kox felt that the students were becoming rowdy in the hallways, she would separate them into two lines (boys and girls) and prepare them to return to their classrooms, sometimes at the expense of the teachers' lunch break.

> Gita has left the teachers' lounge to pick up her students from lunch, but she comes back to warn her colleagues that Mrs. Kox is lining up the students in the hallway. Carrie jokes sarcastically, "Did you tell her I'm not coming back?" The group sighs and laughs at Carrie's joke, but begins to pack up their unfinished lunches.

The teachers often told me that in the past, lunch time had been a kind of recess for the students. However, Kox believed that even the "lunchroom is a place of learning," and she held the teachers accountable for their students' behavior at all times.

Grading

Another way Mrs. Kox tried to deprivatize classroom practices involved the school's grading procedures. In contrast to the previous administrations,

Mrs. Kox required greater accounting of grading practices so students could be monitored and classrooms could be reviewed and compared. She introduced the new procedures early in my fieldwork during a staff meeting.

> I sit with John [teacher] in the multipurpose room and wait for the meeting to begin. As we wait, there is an announcement telling the teachers to bring their "report card packets" to the meeting. As the teachers arrive, John asks one of them, "Did you bring your grade book packet?" The teacher says "Yes" and then jokes sarcastically, "What we need is another form" to document who brought the grading forms and who didn't.
>
> During the meeting, Mrs. Kox refers to the grading packet and says, "We have to monitor the children's progress because too many students are falling through the cracks." As she continues to discuss the new procedures, she adds, "We have to follow students who have failed 2 or 3 years in a row" with district paperwork.
>
> As the meeting ends, a teacher at our table says to her colleagues, "This is unbelievable! Unbelievable!" (in a terse, punctuated whisper with a look of disgust on her face).

The introduction of the new grading procedures continued the following week.

> Mrs. Kox reacquaints the teachers with two forms. One is for a "report card review," and the other for a "grade book review." She tells the teachers that she will review their report cards and grade books and use the forms to give them feedback. For the grade books, Mrs. Kox says that the teachers should have "at least 15 grades per subject." A teacher interjects, "We've never had that much," and it would require two assessments per subject per week, which is "too much assessing" and not enough instruction. Many agree, but Mrs. Kox explains that testing is important because parents often do their children's homework. Then she asks the teachers, "Who wants feedback on this form this quarter?" No one raises their hand.

Mrs. Kox eventually decided not to give the teachers formal "feedback" via the forms. However, she still reviewed the grade books and report cards later that day.

> Mrs. Kox and the assistant principal are reviewing the second-grade report cards, and Kox wonders aloud, "If they are all using the same materials, do the teachers assign the same grades? It's the same curriculum" (implying they should).

As Mrs. Kox continues the review she says, "We should standardize." While looking at a report card she sighs, "Oh, I don't like it."

Mrs. Kox looks at a report card and comments in disbelief, "Oh,
come on! Recognizing numbers one through ten is not introduced
(during the first quarter) in kindergarten?"

Looking at another report card, Mrs. Kox comments, "No,
this is more than I can handle. Why is it [rooms] 231 and
232 have different criteria? Are we teaching the same things to
students?"

Mrs. Kox told me that in the past the grade reviews involved only a "Post-it
note" to signify the administration's approval. Kox's purview of grading was
a discontinuous shift from previous practices, and this shift was unsettling
for many of the teachers. Kox told me that a lot of them were "panicking"
and one was "very worried because she had never seen anyone review her
grade book for the past 26 years."

Curriculum and Instruction

In addition to grading, Mrs. Kox also monitored the school's instructional practices and curriculum. For example, during a staff development day
early in my fieldwork, the staff was supposed to work on creating a standardized curriculum aligned with city and state goals. Echoing accountability, Mrs. Kox told the teachers, "I truly believe every student in Chicago can
succeed." She gave an example of her former school, which "turned it around,"
and the only reason they had struggled in the past "was the curriculum."
Mrs. Kox said that with the right curriculum, even the "difficult" children
could "succeed if you give them the proper support." She implored the teachers to "put the foot down and demand the children learn," because "children know when we lower our expectations."

However, the discussion soon turned to the rigidity of accountability
and the need for autonomy and flexibility. Teachers interjected, "There is a
perception in this school among teachers and students that creativity is limited," and "I agree there should be order, but there has to be some noise with
creativity," and "There has to be a balance with the fluidity required for
creativity." As emotions began to simmer (apparent from looks of disgust
and rising tones and pitches), Mrs. Kox defended her actions (while connecting instruction to student management).

Mrs. Kox said, "If you value running a tight ship," then you have to
have structure, not just in the classroom but also in the hallways and in
the lunchroom. She continued, "I believe in giving children freedom of

control, but until they can control themselves, you can't give them freedom," and "you've got to have order in society."

The issue is control. The teachers were used to individual control, but now Mrs. Kox sought accountability throughout the school. The issue is framed in terms of the students, but the "structure" that Mrs. Kox describes violated the individual autonomy that the teachers had enjoyed in the past.

Despite Mrs. Kox's framing, the teachers struggled to reconcile this change with what they saw as the school's past success. For example, at lunch later that day, a group of teachers were unable to make sense of this change because "the school ran fine before." One of the teachers told a story that exemplified their distress. Speaking with a slight quiver in her hands and lips, she said she was so "freaked out" by accountability that she brought a trash bag to school, tore up the accountability-related paperwork that Mrs. Kox used to monitor instruction into "bits and pieces," put the pieces into the bag, and then "poured chocolate milk over it" to disguise her actions.

To monitor instruction, Mrs. Kox required (and reviewed) daily lesson plans, and she organized a larger instructional review that included an examination of student work.

> Mrs. Kox begins, "Part of my training, my work" is to make sure that instruction is "in alignment with the state and city standards." As a result, "I have a form, a very simple form that I have passed out to you." Mrs. Kox tells teachers that they should fill out the form based on "one period a day," and include "actual work from the children, so I can give you feedback." The teachers are to turn in the form and the examples of student work along with their lesson plans and the rubrics they used for grading. Based on this review, they will "come back and talk about the kinds of assessments we want to do" and create some standardized practices.

At lunch later that day the teachers chafed at this imposition on their autonomy. One of the teachers told her colleagues that she heard that the lesson plans had to correspond exactly with teaching activities on specific days, which was "ridiculous" because teachers have to be "flexible." The other teachers agreed and recalled how lesson plans were originally developed to aid substitute teachers, not to constrain practice.[7]

The frustration increased when the teachers received Mrs. Kox's comments. For example, one of the kindergarten teachers turned in an assignment where students practiced writing upper- and lower-case letters. On the sample of student work, Kox had written, "What's the rubric?" But the teacher was furious and told me, "This is bulls–t," because "this is kinder-garten" and the students are "just learning this letter." She added, "It doesn't have to be like this" because things had run smoothly in the past.

THE TEACHERS' RESPONSE AND THE FATE
OF INSTRUCTIONAL DISCOURSE

No examination of distributed leadership is complete without a discussion of teachers, because teachers can move out of and into the role of follower and, of course, the role of leader (Spillane, Hallett, & Diamond, 2003). As some of the examples discussed above indicate, the teachers at Costen were not docile participants who were willing to follow whoever stood out front. The veteran teachers in particular cherished the autonomy that had characterized the prior school order, and they had a much different view of the situation than the one espoused by Mrs. Kox. These teachers responded to Mrs. Kox's efforts to implement accountability with hostile resentment and by "leading" their own anti-Kox movement—all of which had implications for the practice of leadership at the school.

As some of the examples discussed earlier indicate, many of the teachers were angered by Mrs. Kox's surveillance of their classroom practices. To quote another teacher:

> They [Mrs. Kox's administration] watch over us too much, and I think the staff is capable. When I first came here, the principal we had was never ever [watching them], and this school was supposed to be one of the best schools in Chicago as far as public schools. That is why I can't understand why there is so much people looking over our shoulders.

The previous administrations had high confidence, good faith, and trusted what the teachers were doing behind the closed doors of their classrooms (Meyer & Rowan, 1977). Mrs. Kox's surveillance suggested to many teachers that she did not. The teachers took offense to this, especially in light of their interpretation of the past.

The pace at which Mrs. Kox attempted to implement new organizational routines also angered teachers. For example, during lunch in the teachers' lounge one day, a student teacher said that she could feel a lot of tension in the air, and she asked her mentor why the school had fallen on "tough times." The teacher explained, "She [Kox] made lots of changes, quickly. In most cases, making such quick changes is not good. Mrs. Kox did not follow that code." Other teachers expressed similar sentiments.

Mrs. Kox didn't really take time to look at our school and what the teachers were doing before she changed it. She should have observed before she felt the school needed changing. That wasn't really fair. ... If maybe after a year of observing, then make changes. That would have been more legitimate.

Another teacher put it more simply: "You don't have a baby in a month; it takes 9 months."

The teacher who was most offended by the changes at the school was Mrs. Drew. Mrs. Drew is a highly regarded language arts teacher, and her pedagogical skills are the foundation on which her colleagues pay her considerable respect. Prior to Mrs. Kox's arrival, the students and teachers nominated Mrs. Drew for a prestigious "Golden Apple" award, and she won. In response to Mrs. Kox's actions, Mrs. Drew told me:

What bothered me most is that [Kox] never took the time to figure out what was going on here because she just totally dismantled. And I'm not using hyperbole when I'm using that word "dismantled." She totally dismantled every system that we had. ... And to me, that is the most illogical way to go into any system. ... You first go and see, "Well, what are they doing? How is it working?"

In retrospect, Mrs. Kox admitted that she made changes too fast—she attempted to introduce too many new organizational routines too quickly. At the conclusion of my fieldwork, she told me, "When I came in, I didn't take the time to establish the rapport because I was eager to get the job done." However, Mrs. Kox's attempts were not as "illogical" as Mrs. Drew would contend. Recall that Mrs. Kox came to a school that had no documented history of its previous mode of operation—there were no documents that listed the organizational routines at Costen, and Mrs. Kox was facing a rising tide of accountability that she chose to swim with as opposed to against.

Hindsight is 20/20, but people act in the moment, and Mrs. Drew responded not just with anger, but with organized collective action. Individual acts, more often than not, involve interactions, and it is in these interactions that leadership practice takes shape. In response to Mrs. Kox's actions, a number of teachers had sent anonymous complaint letters to the district office. Mrs. Drew asked the teachers for copies of these letters, and she also encouraged her colleagues to write new complaint letters, which many of them did either individually or in groups. Mrs. Drew compiled all of these complaint letters into a 119-page bound volume, and she titled the book with a play on Mrs. Kox's name: *Turmoil at 'KOX'sten School*. Mrs. Drew made dozens of copies of the book, and she sent it to the school's district office, the regional office, the city's central office, and any other relevant audience she could think of. She explained to me:

> I plastered her [Kox's] name all over this city. Everybody I could think of I sent that book to. And the book was just magnificent. . . . And I compiled letters from the entire staff here and I compiled—it had—oh God, maybe a good 40 odd letters from various teachers. . . . And the title of the book was, a little thing with her name, "Kox," *Turmoil at 'KOX'sten School*. And I sent it all over the city. [After sharing a copy with me, she continues.] And through the whole process, all I kept hearing was, "You can't make principals change. You can't get rid of principals. This is Chicago. Principals are here forever. Let's just ride her out and eventually she'll be gone." I was just like "No, no." The reason it's so difficult to combat leadership is that everybody runs scared.

Mrs. Drew spoke of her effort to "combat leadership," but in effect *she* was also a leader of a teachers' movement against Mrs. Kox's efforts to change the existing order.

Most of the complaint letters criticized Mrs. Kox for trying to change how the school had been organized and for doing so too quickly. For example, one of these letters warned Mrs. Kox:

> Your arrival at Costen is like a person who buys a new house. It is only natural to be anxious to fix it up and make changes that turn your new house into your own home. But in doing so, you should remember that your new "house" already had people living in it. It can be detrimental to the morale of the staff when massive change is forced upon us in a relatively short time—especially when it seems to occur without the benefit of any discernible observations of how things have worked thus far. (Anonymous letter from a group of teachers first sent to Mrs. Kox and then included in *Turmoil at 'KOX'sten School*)

A related criticism decried the increased level of surveillance that came with Mrs. Kox's emphasis on accountability. One letter even went so far as to exclaim, "We feel like we are in a communist country!"

The complaints in the letters were at times reasonable, at times unfair, and often venomous. Mrs. Drew's "book" prompted an investigation of Mrs. Kox by the Chicago Schools' central office. The investigators spent time observing Mrs. Kox, interviewing individual teachers, and having group meetings with the teachers. However, nothing substantive came out of this

investigation because Mrs. Kox never overstepped the bounds of her authority, and she never broke any formal Chicago rules. The investigative team
gave Mrs. Kox a slap on the wrist because she offended the teachers, but
they also gave her a pat on the back because her efforts to change the school
were premised on accountability.

However, the damage was done. Mrs. Kox was quite understandably
paranoid that, as she frequently told me, many of the teachers were "out to
get" her. On the other side, many of the teachers felt deeply wounded by
how Mrs. Kox had attempted to dismantle the previous school order that
they had interpreted as successful. The relational well had been poisoned,
and even the people who tried to stay out of the conflict had to drink the
water. They were pressured to take sides, and even if they refused to do so,
they had to live and work in an increasingly angry atmosphere. It was going
to take a tremendous amount of work to sanitize the well before coopera-
tive relationships would flow forth. The situation illuminates how the interactions, not simply the actions, of individual formal or informal leaders are
the meat and potatoes of leadership practice.

This atmosphere took an emotional toll on everyone. People told me
that the situation was "hard for all of our personal health," that "things are
becoming very frayed at the edges," and "it seems like everyday somebody
else is losing it." When I asked one teacher how she coped, she replied, "I'm
seeing a therapist (laughs), just for work." Despite her laughter, her therapy
was no joke, as she mentioned it frequently. Another teacher recited a litany
of self-help books: *The Natural Mind, Spontaneous Healing*, and *Eight Weeks
to Optimum Health*. This contentious atmosphere also wore on Kox and the
parents of the LSC. Over time I noted that Mrs. Kox had become thinner,
she had frequent colds, and her skin was often pallid. The chair of the LSC
often lamented that he was at the "end of his rope." When I asked him how
he coped with the turmoil at the school, he said, "I don't. I get sick. . . . It
takes a terrible toll on me personally."

Quality of life aside, the painful struggles at the school had implications
for the work of education. After the investigation, it was rare for people at
Costen to talk about the core technology of schooling—instruction. Most of
the available time and energy had to be spent cleaning up and re-establishing
basic relationships between the teachers and the administration, and this
relational drama was stressful. When I asked one teacher how she coped with
the stress, she said, "I close that door. . . . Once I have to open that door and
be part of the bigger community, I—it's difficult and stressful. . . . I don't go
out there much." Many of her colleagues responded in kind. Although the
classroom became a sanctuary, it further isolated teachers from one another
and prevented them from forming a community conducive to instructional
improvement (Purkey & Smith, 1983; Rosenholtz, 1989a). With all that was

going on in the school, I witnessed sustained discourse about instruction on only four occasions, and all of those occasions were during staff development days that were mandated by the Chicago Public Schools.

Everyone at the school suffered, but the real victim of the leadership struggle was instructional discourse. Moreover, it can be argued that the struggles at the school and the fate of instructional discourse affected student achievement: Costen's ITBS reading scores reversed direction. While they had been on a steady rise, on the heels of the investigation of Mrs. Kox, they dropped slightly for the first time in years (from 55.7% reading at or above national norms to 54%).

THE MORAL OF THE STORY:
LESSONS FROM COSTEN SCHOOL

"Leadership struggle" may seem like a contradiction in terms. The very idea of clear-cut "leaders" and "followers" seems to preclude any type of struggle. Moreover, when we think about leadership, we tend to think about its glorious triumph, not the often difficult, even painful, interactions that constitute its development. This is the hidden, sometimes ugly, sometimes pleasant, underside of leadership. It is part of the "dark side" of organizations that too often is neglected in our research (Morrill, Zald, & Rao, 2003; Vaughan, 1999). However, the distributed leadership perspective shines a beam of light into this darkness because it forces us to look into the connections—among leaders, followers, and the situation—and all of the complex relationships therein.

At Costen, the nature of these relations put Mrs. Kox in an incredibly difficult position. She had little knowledge of the social order that prevailed at the school before her arrival, so she had little footing on which to build relationships with the teachers. Moreover, city and state policy (as well as her own beliefs) compelled her to quickly introduce accountability into the school. However, this accountability was at odds with the autonomy that the teachers were used to and that they felt had produced results in the past. As a middle manager, Mrs. Kox was being held to account as well. But the teachers, the very people on whom Mrs. Kox's success depended, were offended by her efforts to increase accountability. They refused to follow, and their own efforts to lead a movement against Mrs. Kox resulted in an investigation of Kox. The struggle to deal with all of these tensions was painful for everyone.

The leadership struggle at Costen Elementary teaches us that leadership is not inherent in organizational positions. Simply because someone holds a position as a school principal does not mean that teachers will follow his or her lead, and simply because someone is in the position of a teacher does not mean that he or she cannot be a leader. This point may seem trite, but it has been somewhat lost in recent accountability policies. In many ways, accountability policies are an effort to formalize schools as organizations. They are premised on rational-legal models of positional authority, and they increase the centralization of schools by creating standards that are enforced by a line of school authorities, from the CEO of the Chicago Schools to the central office to the regional offices to individual school principals and their subordinates. In holding schools accountable for student performance, these mechanisms attempt to create a tighter connection between educational policy and instructional practices where loose connections had been the norm (Meyer & Rowan, 1977; Weick, 1976).

Mrs. Kox acted in ways that fit this accountability model. If the assumptions about the nature of authority in the accountability model were right, we would expect teachers to comply because they were Kox's subordinates. But life in schools is never this simple. Despite Mrs. Kox's formal authority, many of the teachers never saw her as a credible leader, and they refused to follow. As a result, when Mrs. Kox used her authority in an effort to crack open classrooms and deprivatize instruction, the emergent struggle resulted in *more* closed doors as teachers tried to escape the controversy, and *less* instructional discourse. Even though Mrs. Kox used her authority to make changes with the intention of increasing test scores, in the emergent struggle test scores *declined*.

While some of the particulars of the leadership struggle at Costen School may be extraordinary, this kind of situation is not that unusual, especially for new principals who are intent on changing standard organizational routines in their schools. Nor is Costen the only school that faces external accountability pressures that clash with local autonomy. With the passage of federal No Child Left Behind (NCLB) legislation, many schools find themselves in a similar situation. In this sense, there are many "Costen Schools," there are many "Mrs. Koxes," and there are many "Costen teachers."

What can be done to ease the tensions of the leadership struggle? As Mrs. Kox admitted in retrospect, she could have taken more time to establish a rapport with the teachers before introducing change. However, this would have necessitated holding off accountability policies while risking the wrath of the LSC and the district office. Time is exactly what principals *lack* in the era of high-stakes accountability, and the clock continues to tick against Costen (and many other schools). At the same time that Costen's reading scores on the ITBS dipped for the first time in years, a school in the same neighborhood with the same student population outpaced Costen by eight points in reading and seven in math. Kox and her superiors were well aware of this comparison, which created greater accountability pressure. These pressures were exacerbated by the federal NCLB policies that were created after I finished my fieldwork. Even though Costen's test scores rebounded at the end of my fieldwork and rose in the following years, under the first year of NCLB (2003–04), Costen was already failing to meet "adequate yearly progress" toward goals in seven areas.[8] Although NCLB policies have many provisions to exempt schools, "needing time to establish the human relationships on which leadership depends" is not one of them.

Accountability is not the only approach that has a myopic view of leadership. "Leader-centric" models have long characterized the literature (Likert, 1967; Mouton & Blake, 1984; White & Lippitt, 1960; Yukl, 1981). In contrast, Meindl (1995) and others argue that to understand leadership, we must focus on how followers construct leaders and not on leaders per se. In this view, leadership is in the eye of the beholder. However, this "follower-centered" approach is still too narrow because it downplays the substance on which followers construct others as leaders (Spillane, Hallett, & Diamond, 2003), and how the construction of leadership evolves as a product of ongoing social interactions (Ehrlich, 1998; Schneider, 1998).

Just as leadership is not affixed to a position or to specific people, it is not equivalent to a set of actions, even when those actions are informed by "best practices." Based on research on what scholars already deemed as "successful" cases of leadership, a growing literature argues that the principal should engage in a particular set of practices. The principal is to set the tone for instruction by creating an instructional vision and by monitoring classrooms, and he or she should promote the formation of "instructional communities" by deprivatizing classroom practices as a way to make instruction transparent and public, and creating opportunities for teachers to talk together about the challenges inherent in their work. In many ways, these were the very things that Mrs. Kox tried to do. However, these practices did not fit the norm of teacher autonomy that was an important part of the situation at Costen, and the teachers reacted against these practices instead of following along. To be sure, practice is a part of leadership, but these practices are always embedded in the relationship among leaders, followers, and the situation. Principal practice alone is not sufficient for success because leadership is a distributed phenomenon that takes shape in the interactions. The leadership struggle at Costen School teaches us that "best practices" and accountability policies are not a cure-all because they are only part of a bigger relational picture.

6

The Practice of Leadership in Mathematics and Language Arts: The Adams Case

Jennifer Zoltners Sherer
UNIVERSITY OF PITTSBURGH

Schools are under increasing pressure from all sides to show improvement in student performance on standardized tests in language arts, mathematics, and soon, science. More and more, we see policies that use student performance on standardized tests to hold schools accountable. Many school districts have implemented initiatives that tie student promotion to performance on standardized tests. Some also have tied school operating procedures to student test performance, taking over schools that consistently underperform on standardized tests. New federal policy initiatives such as No Child Left Behind use standardized test results as one measure with which to judge school progress. Schools that accept Reading First grants agree to administer a series of standardized tests as required documentation of progress in student learning. Discussions of these policy levers rarely take the school subject into account; it is assumed that high-stakes accountability policies will influence how schools respond to and work toward implementing instruction in the same way regardless of the school subject.

In this chapter, I use a distributed leadership framework to investigate one school's response to a high-stakes testing environment. More specifically, I examine school leaders' response in the form of a new organizational routine designed to improve instruction with the purpose of increasing test scores in mathematics, reading, and writing. Because organizational routines are a key mechanism through which leaders enact their practice, they offer an important window into leadership practice in schools. Through a case study of the Five-Week Assessment routine at Adams School from 2000–2003, I examine similarities and differences in leadership and managment practice related to mathematics and language arts in one elementary school.

The Five-Week Assessment routine, as designed by school leaders at Adams, was similar in mathematics and language arts. Both routines had common origins and goals, and they shared similar input and output components such as standards, curriculum guides, and standardized tests. The routines as enacted in day-to-day life at Adams, however, were different. In practice, school leaders prioritized language arts activities over mathematics. Leadership practice in mathematics was different from that in language arts in at least two distinct ways. First, the ways in which leaders used tools was static in mathematics and dynamic in language arts. Second, the social networks that evolved around the language arts routine were denser than those in mathematics, with participants interacting more frequently with more people in language arts. In some respects, leadership practice at Adams was consistent with epistemological differences in mathematics and language arts.

Leadership practice was very different in mathematics as opposed to language arts. Through the tightly controlled pacing of a standardized textbook and a weakly supported routine, leadership practice related to mathematics was linear and sequential. Math leaders created a clear plan for teachers to move sequentially through a standard textbook, and there was little to no wavering from that plan. The path to math learning was a straight shot from point A (teach students the textbook in this prescribed order) to point B (student performance will improve on the standardized tests). Leadership practice for language arts, on the other hand, was more fluid and open to change. While language arts leaders also created a plan for teachers, this plan involved a variety of curricular materials and frequent opportunities for teachers to discuss language arts instruction. There were multiple paths to student learning in language arts, with curves and turns along the way.

UNDERSTANDING ORGANIZATIONAL ROUTINES

I use a distributed framework to study leadership and management practice at Adams School. Focusing on leadership practice, I investigate not only the people involved in leadership work, but also the tools that they used and the way that practice was stretched over leaders, followers, and elements of the situation. In order to study the practice of leading and managing, I focus analysis on organizational routines, as much of the work of organizations gets done in routines. I also consider the tools leaders used as they constructed and implemented the Five-Week Assessment routine, the sources of those tools, and the social networks that developed around the routine. In addition to the distributed framework, I use work on organizational routines, organizational theory, and subject matter as a context for work in schools to interpret my findings.

Organizational routines are an important part of organizational work (Feldman, 2000; Feldman & Pentland, 2003; March, 1981; March & Simon, 1958). By organizational routines, I mean "repetitive, recognizable patterns of interdependent actions, carried out by multiple actors" (Feldman & Pentland, 2003, p. 95). Much of the work of schools, in common with other organizations, happens through multiple organizational routines. Feldman and Pentland (2003) view routines as having both *ostensive* and *performative* aspects. With routines, the *ostensive aspect* is the idea of the routine—"the ideal or schematic form of a routine. It is the abstract, generalized idea of the routine. . . . The *performative aspect* of the routine consists of specific actions, by specific people, in specific places and times. It is the routine in practice" (p. 101). The ostensive aspect acts as a script for the routine. The performative aspect is the routine in practice—its performance in a particular place and time.

Contingency theory suggests that organizational features vary depending on the degree to which the task environment is defined. In environments where the tasks are well defined and not variable, a classic bureaucratic type of organization is more appropriate, whereas in organizations where the tasks are variable and not well defined, a more participatory organization is more appropriate (Perrow, 1967). Building on this work, Rowan (1990, 2002a, 2002b) describes two organizational designs of schools: commitment and control. In the *control* model, teaching is viewed as a well-defined, nonvariable activity. In response to this, leaders develop a standardized system of input, behavior, and output controls that constrains teachers' methods and content decisions. When teaching is viewed as a complex technology, the *commitment* model seems more appropriate. Characteristics of a commitment model include teacher participation in decision making, network structures of professional control, collegiality among teachers, and the development of community within the school. Rowan views these models as incompletely implemented in schools, although they work best when applied intensively.

While many researchers see subject matter as an important context for teachers' work (Ball & Lacey, 1995; Little, 1995a, 1995b; McLaughlin & Talbert, 1993; Siskin, 1991a, 1991b, 1994; Stodolsky & Grossman, 1995; Talbert, 1995), few look at subject matter as it pertains to elementary teachers, and fewer still as it pertains to school leadership (Burch & Spillane, 2003, 2005; Cobb & McClain, 2005; Knapp, Grossman, & Stodolsky, 2005; Spillane,

2006; Spillane & Burch, 2004, 2006; Stein & D'Amico, 1999, 2002). With the exception of Stodolsky's (1988) work, which demonstrates how elementary teachers treat subject matter differently within their own classrooms, there is little research on how subject matters structure teachers' work. School subjects have different epistemologies, and this enables and constrains the ways in which teachers and leaders build their practice. Consequently, leaders may approach reform of instruction in these subject areas differently. It is from this place that my study begins.

I engaged in an intensive investigation of leadership practice at Adams School over three consecutive school years beginning in 2000, returning the fourth year to reflect on my findings with school personnel. I spent an average of 3 days per month at the school for 3 of these years (2000–2003). In an effort to capture a complete picture of leadership practice and the Five-Week Assessment routine, I collected a variety of data (Table 6.1).

Using the coding software Nudist, I systematically coded all interviews, leader shadows, field notes, and meeting data for evidence of the performative and ostensive aspects of the Five-Week Assessment routine in mathematics and language arts. By content coding as a first cut through the data, I was able to define the routines and identify patterns that characterized each routine. I looked at how and where the routine emerged in the work of the school and the practice of leaders and teachers. I found evidence of the routine consistently framing the leader talk, leader activity, and follower activity. I looked for patterns across these content codes, using my theoretical framework as a guide to inform new chunks. These codes include roles, tools, and social networks. I often represent patterns with examples from a second-grade teacher's experience—that of Ms. Matthews—during the course of the 2001–02 school year.

Table 6.1. Data Collected

Type of data	1999–00	2000–01	2001–02	2002–03
Formal leader interviews	5	8	21	12
Informal leader interviews	0	10	8	5
Formal teacher interviews	6	9	15	9
Informal teacher interviews	0	1	23	3
Leader shadows	0	3	7	0
Field notes	0	7	42	8
Meeting observations	5	9	28	9

THE IMPORTANCE OF ROUTINES

Leadership and management practice is enacted in great part through organizational routines. In 1989, a new principal, Dr. Williams, took over a struggling Adams Elementary, a K–8 public school in Chicago. From 2000–2003, it served more than 1,000 students, over 90% of whom were predominantly African American and low-income (97% qualified for free or reduced-price lunch), with a high mobility rate (35%). When Dr. Williams arrived at Adams, the staff—housed in two buildings—was fragmented. Many teachers shut their doors and taught in isolation, having little to no connection with their colleagues. Standardized test scores were low in mathematics and reading. In the face of these challenges, and with pressure from new district policies, Dr. Williams set out to improve test scores and build a collaborative faculty. She developed and got buy-in for her instructional vision through the creation of a series of new, interconnected routines. With the assistance of Ms. Tracy, a former colleague with literacy expertise whom she hired to act as her literacy coordinator, Dr. Williams built a series of organizational routines defined below. (The development of these routines is discussed in Chapter 3.)

- *Breakfast Club.* A series of monthly morning meetings, often led by teachers, to discuss recent research. Teachers discussed journal articles together (primarily literacy-related) as they ate breakfast provided by Dr. Williams.
- *Teacher Leader.* The faculty voted to lengthen the school days so they could have a monthly half day for professional development sessions. Instead of bringing in outside "expertise" to lead these professional development meetings, Dr. Williams tapped into the strengths of her faculty, and the teachers taught one another in these professional development sessions.
- *Content-Focused Groups.* Two smaller groups—the Literacy Committee and the Math Team—met to plan language arts and mathematics activities, discuss classroom practice, and reflect on progress made and desired.
- *Five-Week Assessment.* The Five-Week Assessment was the one routine that directly connected to standardized testing. Every 5 weeks, students were assessed in reading, writing, and mathematics. The assessments provided an opportunity for students to gain practice with test taking. The assessments also provided a frequent opportunity for leaders to get the pulse of the highly mobile student body, looking at these student data to identify strengths and weaknesses. Leaders used this information to plan various leadership tasks, including topics for Breakfast Club and Teacher

Leader meetings. The routine also provided formative assessment data that the teachers could then use to improve their instruction.

While leaders designed these routines to be interdependent, each was able to function without the others. However, the routines in practice often intertwined, informing one another. For example, needs that were identified through the student assessment data in the Five-Week Assessment routine informed the focus of upcoming meetings or professional development sessions. These routines were intended to improve student learning in reading, writing, and mathematics through focused assessments, teacher empowerment, internal professional development, and multiple opportunities for teachers to talk about research and practice. While the Breakfast Club focused primarily on language arts, the other routines were designed to support instruction in both mathematics and language arts.

In the 1990s, the district implemented a high-stakes testing initiative focused on grades 3, 6, and 8 in mathematics and reading. Students in those grades were promoted to the next grade only upon scoring at a certain level on the Iowa Test of Basic Skills (ITBS) in mathematics and reading, and schools also were judged based on student performance in reading, writing, and mathematics. Underperforming schools were put on probation and threatened with being reconstituted. This initiative was modified several years after implementation (Roderick & Nagaoka, 2004), but the overall response of schools was to increase their focus on improving test scores, and Adams School was no exception. The ways in which school leaders reacted to this focus differed. In the late 1990s, the district shifted its accountability focus toward the Illinois Standard Achievement Test (ISAT), which included writing as well as higher order thinking skills in reading and mathematics (Easton et al., 2003). School leaders' organizational responses to low achievement during the first half of the 1990s, and the district-level accountability policy in the second half of that decade, form the backdrop for my discussion of the Five-Week Assessment routine.

DESIGNED ROUTINE

Common Origins: The Five-Week Assessment Routine in Mathematics and Language Arts

School leaders designed the Five-Week Assessment routine in mathematics and language arts to be similar in purpose and goals; the routine had identical origins for both subjects. In response to feedback from a 1996 visit by Board of Education members, Dr. Williams and Ms. Tracy sought to create a routine that would help them answer two related questions: "Are the children learning? And, how do you know?" They developed the Five-Week Assessment routine to answer these questions and to provide students with practice taking standardized tests. In the routine, all students in grades 1–8 took an assessment in mathematics, reading, and writing every 5 weeks. School leaders built this routine in mathematics and language arts with the same goals in mind: They wanted to know what their students were learning in order to better target their efforts. Dr. Williams and Ms. Tracy identify the goals of the routine as follows:

> I think that they [teachers] finally began to look at the assessment as a tool for letting them know what they need to work on in the classroom. That was the goal. . . . It was the test scores, and the reporting of the test scores, that was the big motivation.
> (Dr. Williams, 2000)

> We [the principal and I] were just discussing our school, what was taking place, and what would help the children achieve at a higher level. We were talking about teachers, and we were just kind of casually saying that for the majority of our teachers they all work very hard. But some of them get very low results when it comes to these achievement tests. And we were trying to figure out why, and we decided that they were working hard, most of them, but they were not working smart. From there we decided not to ask anymore, "Are the teachers working," but, "Are the children learning?" So this was a way to find out: Are they learning? (Ms. Tracy)

Table 6.2 shows the ostensive aspect of the Five-Week Assessment routine, as gleaned from interview data. As designed, the cycle repeated every 5 weeks throughout the school year. School leaders typically enacted steps 1 and 2 before the beginning of each school year, and they integrated steps 3–8 roughly every 5 weeks throughout the school year.

Language Arts Five-Week Assessment Routine. The routine involved a 5-week cycle. In order to identify the designed aspect of the routine, I gleaned details from the ways in which leaders talked about the routine. Ms. Tracy described her first step in the routine: "We look at the standards, the Illinois standards and the city standards and goals. And we look at what they want the children to accomplish for the year. And then I kind of back up from that and set up a testing program that matches that." She used tools to help her determine what the students should learn. Ms. Tracy then created a schedule for the reading and writing assessments and wrote the actual assessments

Table 6.2. The Five-Week Assessment Routine as Designed (Ostensive Aspect, Fall 2000)

Step 1	Identify needs
Step 2	Plan Five-Week Assessment routine
Step 3	Develop assessments
Step 4	Copy and distribute assessments
Step 5	Administer and return assessments
Step 6	Score assessments
Step 7	Compile and analyze scores
Step 8	Share scores and identify needs

that were distributed to students. "First there's a selection of tests, and it's not done haphazardly. I actually read and consider what I want the students to be able to pull out of the story because I have to make sure it's there for each grade level."

Three years later, a new literacy coordinator, Ms. Kelly, described this same needs-analysis step. She used a slightly different tool to guide her assessment design. She described, "I gather the Five-Week Assessments, and they're all basically based on the ISAT tests." In both cases, the literacy coordinator used external tools—standards and standardized tests—to develop the assessment plan. Every 5 weeks, the literacy coordinator and her assistant distributed the assessments. Once the teachers had given the assessments, they returned them to the literacy coordinator and her assistant, who scored the assessments and then compiled and analyzed the data.

In the first year of the routine, the literacy coordinator shared the results with the principal. They noted that there was no difference in student performance as compared with the previous year, before the routine was enacted. They realized, as Dr. Williams noted, "what was missing was we didn't find time for the teachers to talk about the results of the Five-Week Assessment." They believed that this feedback loop was crucial, and they added that to the designed routine.

Mathematics Five-Week Assessment Routine. A different set of school leaders created the same Five-Week Assessment routine in mathematics. In the late 1990s, the math coordinator at Adams ran the routine in a similar way to the literacy coordinator. According to her assistant, the math coordinator selected, copied, and distributed the assessments, collecting and compiling scores at the end of each 5-week cycle. While she did not have a feedback loop to teachers, she did meet with the principal to discuss results and develop a mathematics plan for each year. When she left the school in the fall of 2000, the principal appointed four teachers to the Math Team to take over leadership responsibilities in mathematics. While the routine was no longer centralized around one person, the principal expected the Math Team, with the help of the math assistant, to take over the tasks of the routine. She explained:

> [The Math Team] will help with the assessments. [I have] a teacher assistant who helps with some of the paperwork. . . . But what we do is if there's a need to free [Math Team] teachers up, I do that. We budget with sub money so that I can free them up or, you know, they've had some meetings after school. So we just have to be more flexible with the design for them.

The Routine as Part of a Control Organization

In some ways the Five-Week Assessment routine, as designed, is characteristic of a control organization. A control organization is characterized by "a standardized system [with] clear input, behavior, and output controls that constrain teachers' methods and content decisions, control student access to content, and assure exposure to a standardized quality of instruction" (Rowan, 1990, p. 358). In the case of Adams, *input controls* included standardized tests, standards, pacing guides, and topic lists. As stated earlier, the literacy coordinator used standards and standardized tests to frame their design of the assessments. Additionally, leaders at Adams created pacing guides in mathematics and topic lists in language arts that identified the content focus of each Five-Week Assessment. The Math Team created a pacing guide by generating a timeline for coverage of the standard math textbook at each grade level. They used a school calendar and added in extra days so that the teachers could teach all of the material prescribed in the time frame allotted. The literacy coordinator also created a guide, but rather than create a pacing guide based on a standard curriculum, she built a topic list consisting of areas of instructional focus for each 5-week cycle. See Table 6.3 for examples.

At the beginning of the school year, leaders distributed an item-analysis of the Iowa Test of Basic Skills in mathematics and reading. This item-analysis was to be used by teachers to drive classroom instruction. The principal explained the document at a faculty meeting in August 2001, after distributing it to the staff.

Table 6.3. Input Controls in Mathematics and Language Arts

Assessment	Date	Mathematics (2nd grade)	Language Arts (2nd grade)
5-week	September	ITBS practice test	ISAT practice test
10-week	October	Chapters 1–4 cumulative test	Graphic organizers, Descriptive writing
15-week	December	Chapters 5–7 cumulative test	Reading comprehension, Narrative writing
20-week	January	Chapters 8–10 cumulative test	Reading comprehension, Narrative writing

This is a breakdown of the Iowa test skills analysis. It is a breakdown of the percentage of questions that are being asked in every tested area. We took it a step further. And we not only gave you the percentage, but we actually gave you the number of questions that are being asked in each testing area. And this is all of the four major areas—reading, mathematics, science, and social studies. It's right here! It has been broken down the same exact way. So you may want to use this to help guide your planning so that we don't have to wait up until test time to start planning and teaching test-taking techniques and skills and all of those things. If we do it from the beginning, in April or May, or whenever those tests are given, our children should have a pretty good handle on what is expected of them.

The *output controls* in the Five-Week Assessment routine were the assessments given every 5 weeks within the routine and the annual standardized tests. While the *behavior controls* connected to the Five-Week Assessment routine are not as clear at Adams School as in a traditional bureaucratic control organization, there was professional development at Adams in mathematics and language arts that served, in some form, this behavior-control function. Teacher Leader sessions often involved professional development in reading, writing, mathematics, or general teaching strategies.

The leaders' intention for the Five-Week Assessment routine was to get regular snapshots of student learning, respond with relevant professional development and resource support, and improve student scores on high-stakes standardized tests. While the goal, frequency, and purpose of the Five-Week Assessment routine was the same in mathematics and language arts, the ways in which the routine was enacted or performed—and the influence that enactment had on instructional practice—varied by school subject.

THE ROUTINE IN PRACTICE

Subject-Matter Differences: Dynamic and Static Uses of Tools

There are several important similarities and differences in the ways in which school leaders and teachers enacted the Five-Week Assessment routine in mathematics and language arts. One important aspect of the distributed leadership frame is that the tools leaders use are a critical component of leadership practice, framing and focusing interactions among teachers and leaders. In this section, I consider tools and the ways in which leaders use similar tools differently across the two subjects. Specifically, I discuss differences in the routines through the lens of a control organization (inputs, outputs, and behavior controls). I primarily use second-grade teacher Ms. Matthews's experiences to view these differences. Ms. Matthews was the math leader for her grade level and became a member of the Math Team in 2001. I then analyze how these differences had an impact on leadership practice in mathematics and language arts at Adams School.

Input Controls. The inputs in the mathematics and language arts routines are quite similar. In both subjects, teachers have a variety of tools to use as they build their practice: curricular materials, pacing guides (mathematics) and topic lists (language arts), standards, and the ITBS item-analysis. Despite these similarities in input controls, teachers and school leaders used them differently in mathematics and language arts.

In mathematics, the teachers used a standardized set of curricular materials, while in language arts they used a variety of resources. Ms. Matthews designed mathematics lesson plans for her grade-level colleagues that directly followed the textbook. She passed them out to her colleagues, but they rarely discussed them. As Ms. Matthews explained:

> We [the second-grade team] haven't really [met about mathematics] yet. . . . I think they pretty much, it's pretty easy. I just follow the book. I do an activity with [the students] to start out like to warm them up. And then you go in and do the page together and then they do it on their own for practice.

Her opinion indicates both that math is straightforward and that her practice is closely tied to the textbook. The teachers' and leaders' dependence on the textbook may be a result of past success in using the textbook. In the mid-1990s, school leaders adopted new mathematics and language arts textbooks. While standardized test scores improved in mathematics after the textbook adoption, they did not in reading.

In language arts, the use of curricular materials extended beyond a standard textbook. Across the school, leaders provided teachers with a range of different materials with which to teach reading and writing. For instance, some third-grade teachers utilized a highly structured phonics program, Metro, while their colleagues used stories from Harcourt Brace and created research projects on animals and the solar system that they crafted in collaboration with the librarian. Literacy leaders like the reading lead teacher in her grade level (Ms. Manny) and the literacy coordinator (Ms. Kelly) sought Ms. Matthews out in free moments and grade-level meetings to discuss language arts lesson plans and strategies. For example, early one October morning, Ms. Matthews and Ms. Manny discussed reading instruction. Ms. Manny shared with Ms. Matthews what she did with her students the day before and made recommendations to Ms. Matthews, who was introducing the story that day. Ms. Matthews planned to introduce her students to graphic organizers, and she asked for Ms. Manny's help in deciding which graphic organizer would go best with the story she was planning to read with her students.

In addition to curriculum materials, teachers used the pacing guides/topic lists differently in mathematics and language arts. Teachers used the mathematics pacing guide as a static tool. They did not stray from the guide, teaching in the order that the guide dictated. Conversely, teachers used the topic list in language arts as a flexible and dynamic tool that guided rather than prescribed their practice.

In the beginning of the year, the Math Team was clear in communicating their expectation that the teachers must hold to the schedule. For this reason, the math leaders felt there was no excuse for teachers to be behind schedule. Ms. Jones, a Math Team member, explained:

> First of all, [teachers need to] get focused on that time frame that we set up because a lot of teachers are not following that time frame. . . . When we first met after the first 5 weeks, one teacher said she was only done—now you should be done with Chapters 1–4—she was only done with Chapter 1. Come on now. In 5 weeks? No, that's not acceptable to me. But you know, these—some of [the teachers] have low expectations for these [students]—"Well these kids can't do and they're—and I don't want to push." Yes, you have to push these kids and tell them what they're capable of doing. People have been telling them so long what they can't do, tell them what they can do. And then if you're going with them, you're going down to their level instead of bringing them up to your level.

In some ways, the rigidity of this pacing schedule created a situation in which the teachers were teaching the material, and not the students. Teachers must balance the rigidity of the math leaders' demands, as reified in the pacing guide, with skills their students come in with, teacher expectations, and so on. In mathematics, the input control was clear and well defined. The teachers all followed the same textbook and used the pacing guide written by the Math Team to direct their teaching. When they fell behind, they were expected by the mathematics leadership to give the scheduled assessment anyway, even if they had not covered all of the material.

In language arts, the topic list was less rigidly defined and was not always followed by the teachers. The topic list broadly defined concepts to teach rather than specific material to cover ("reading comprehension" vs. Chapters 1–4 of a textbook) and left more room for teacher interpretation and choice of instructional materials (see Table 6.3). This can be seen in the diversity of materials Ms. Matthews drew on in her language arts teaching— ideas from her colleagues for writing prompts and graphic organizers, a project she created with the librarian, and so on. The language arts topic list was created by the literacy coordinator at the beginning of the year, but unlike the math pacing guide, there were times when it changed. One example of this is when the teachers voted, in an October 2000 literacy committee meeting, on what the focus for the next 5 weeks should be in reading, based on current student needs. This flexibility was not consistent; at times the topic list drove the content for each reading and writing cycle. Although the input controls in language arts were inconsistent, teachers were able to use them in more dynamic ways, responsive to the needs of students and teachers. Conversely, in mathematics leaders built input controls that were directive. While teachers may have been slower than the pacing guide dictated, they used the input controls in more rigid ways by following the prescribed sequence.

Output Controls. The output controls, by design, were similar in the mathematics and language arts routines. Data from the Five-Week Assessments gave leaders a snapshot of schoolwide student performance in mathematics, reading, and writing. This allowed them to design their professional development and allocate resources into areas of greatest need. School leaders also could feed back the data to teachers to use as formative assessment to design the focus of their classroom instruction in mathematics, reading, and writing. In practice, the use of these data varied widely. From time to time, the literacy leaders used the assessment data to improve instruction. However, these data were never used in this way in the mathematics routine.

An important component of the routine is the feedback loop; assessment information collected every 5 weeks was intended to inform instruction. In order for the teachers to use these formative data, someone had to compile and analyze them. This task was designed into the routine as a leader responsibility, and the leaders did, in most cases, collect the scores. But they were inconsistent in analyzing and disseminating that analysis to teachers. In some cases, the literacy coordinator and her assistant compiled the scores and discussed them with the principal, assistant principals, and teachers in various formats: written memos, grade-level meetings, and individual conferences with teachers. Other times, the reading and writing scores were collected and not analyzed. Reasons for this include the logistical inability of the literacy coordinator and her assistant to score and analyze the scores in a timely manner, and the inability to create time to meet with teachers to give feedback. Both stumbling blocks resulted from resource issues commonly found in schools: a lack of time and money.

The scores in mathematics were collected at times. In 2001–02, the literacy coordinator's assistant entered the mathematics scores into a computer program. In 2002–03, a math leader in the K–3 building (Ms. Brown) compiled—by hand—all of the student scores for grades 1–3. Ms. Brown spent some time analyzing the data, but I found no evidence of feedback of these data to math teachers from 2000–2003.

Behavior Controls. Behavior controls include inservice training for effective teaching practices and formal evaluation tied to how frequently teachers implement these effective practices (Rowan, 1990, 2002a, 2002b). A common form of behavior control is a walk through. These typically involve a small team of teachers and leaders informally dropping into classrooms for short visits. While Ms. Kelly identified her reading team and their intention to do periodic walk throughs, they did not have a plan as to how they would provide coverage in order to include teachers on the walk through. While the principal did formal evaluations of the classrooms, these were infrequent and general. There were no formal behavior controls specifically tied to the Five-Week Assessment routine in either mathematics or language arts.

There is, however, evidence of some informal behavior control tied to the Five-Week Assessment routine. In mathematics professional development sessions at Adams, math leaders told teachers how to teach in two ways: Leaders led teachers through sample lessons, and leaders shared with teachers what they did in their own classrooms. In my discourse analysis of mathematics meetings, I found that math leaders predominantly spoke about monitoring the improvement effort, sharing resources, sharing what they did in their classrooms, and inviting others to speak, while math teachers primarily asked clarifying questions. Teachers at Adams talked infrequently about ideas in mathematics, and they did not identify problems and develop solutions to those problems, nor did they collaborate around mathematics practice like they did in language arts. Because the teachers rarely engaged in math discussions, math Teacher Leader sessions often involved math teacher leaders telling other math teachers how to teach mathematics.

Conversely, professional development sessions in language arts took various forms. Monthly Breakfast Club meetings provided teachers with the opportunity to talk about reading instruction through the lens of recent research. Language arts meetings provided teachers with opportunities to learn new strategies and also talk about their own ideas, problems, and solutions. Discourse analysis of language arts meetings shows that, unlike in mathematics, leaders presented a broad vision for language arts, offered strategies in response to teachers' self-identified needs, offered expertise and resources, and encouraged collaboration. Teachers identified needs, goals, and strategies, and they shared their classroom practice. While professional development in language arts had some elements of leaders telling teachers how to teach, these same teachers (who taught both mathematics and language arts) engaged more in discussions about language arts than they did about mathematics.

Despite similar input and output controls in the mathematics and language arts Five-Week Assessment routines, the ways in which teachers and leaders used these controls varied. Additionally, different informal behavior controls were enacted in mathematics and language arts.

Differences: Connected versus Fragmented Social Networks

The interconnected and sequential nature of the Five-Week Assessment routine made it possible for social networks to build. Extensive differences existed between the social networks that leaders and teachers formed in mathematics and language arts around this routine. As compared with the frequent and dynamic social network in language arts, math leaders and teachers rarely communicated with one another about the routine. These differences influenced the ways in which leaders and teachers did their work.

Many aspects of the Five-Week Assessment routine involved communication. As designed, the routine involved the work of multiple individuals, and it connected the work of all students, teachers, and leaders at Adams. A look at Ms. Matthews's participation in the social networks around subject matter, and the Five-Week Assessment routine in particular, reflects differences in the language arts and mathematics social networks. Over the course of a year's observations, Ms. Matthews's practice connected with others four times in mathematics, two that directly related to the routine. In a meeting in August, Ms. Jones introduced the changes to the mathematics routine by introducing the mathematics pacing guide. The second connection relating to the routine happened when Ms. Brown, a Math Team member, periodically brought Ms. Matthews the assessments to give her students. Three people were involved in these connections—the classroom teacher, the building math leader, and the school math leader (see Figure 6.1).

In language arts, by contrast, Ms. Matthews had six connection points, five of which were directly related to the routine. She collaborated with colleagues around classroom lessons and units three times and attended three meetings where language arts-related topics were discussed. As mentioned earlier, Ms. Matthews got reading advice about how to use graphic organizers from Ms. Manny. En route to an after-school meeting one afternoon, Ms. Matthews, Ms. Manny, and the second-grade writing lead teacher Ms. Smithman talked about their ideas for teaching persuasive writing, the focus of the current 5-week writing cycle. Ms. Smithman shared ideas for writing prompts and writing lessons she and the literacy coordinator recently had discussed. In an August meeting, the literacy coordinator explained the changes to the Five-Week Assessment routine. In an October Literacy Committee meeting, the faculty voted on the next focus of the language arts Five-Week Assessment routine. Finally, the literacy coordinator called a second-grade meeting in January to discuss how they should step up their writing instruction, since their students were very behind. Their students were still writing one- or two-paragraph papers, while the second-grade students at another public school she recently visited were writing five-paragraph essays. The literacy coordinator was convinced that their students could do better, and having them do so would take pressure off the third-grade teachers (whose students were at a benchmark year). The literacy coordinator emphasized that if the second-grade teachers did a better job of pushing their students in writing, then more third-grade students would achieve passing scores in writing. She passed out two documents she had created: The first document had suggestions for teaching a three-paragraph essay, and the other document detailed important elements of persuasive writing. In language arts, Ms. Matthews connected with a large number of people about the routine.

Ms. Matthews's experience is typical of teachers at Adams. In fact, because she became a math leader for the building and was a math leader for her grade-level team, the interactions she had around mathematics may have been more frequent than those of other teachers. One exception to this may be a teacher who is uncomfortable in mathematics and seeks out advice on a frequent basis to help alleviate concerns. However, I found no evidence of this. In fact, even a teacher with no previous experience teaching mathematics was not overly concerned with starting to teach mathematics mid-year.

Overall data (interview and observation) show that the social network connected with the mathematics routine was weak overall and was fragmented across the two buildings that made up the school. Ms. Brown distributed assessments to every first- through third-grade teacher. These teachers returned

Figure 6.1. Ms. Matthews's Interactions Around Mathematics and Language Arts

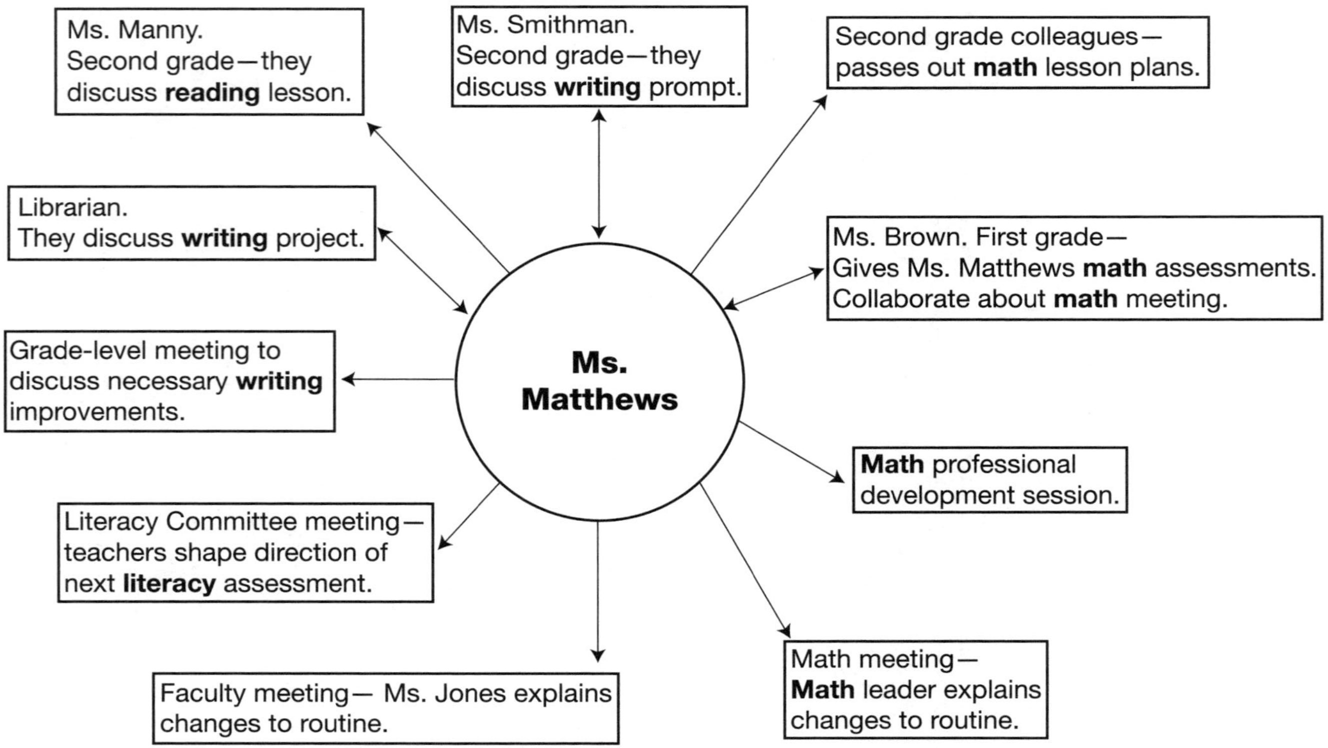

Second grade colleagues—passes out **math** lesson plans.

Ms. Brown. First grade—Gives Ms. Matthews **math** assessments. Collaborate about **math** meeting.

Math professional development session.

Math meeting—**Math** leader explains changes to routine.

Ms. Smithman. Second grade—they discuss **writing** prompt.

Ms. Manny. Second grade—they discuss **reading** lesson.

Librarian. They discuss **writing** project.

Grade-level meeting to discuss necessary **writing** improvements.

Literacy Committee meeting—teachers shape direction of next **literacy** assessment.

Faculty meeting— Ms. Jones explains changes to routine.

Ms. Matthews

their mathematics scores to either the literacy coordinator's assistant or Ms. Brown. While Math Team members led several professional development sessions each year, these sessions were not directly related to the routine (see Figure 6.2).

In comparison, the social network around the language arts routine was centralized around the literacy coordinator (see Figure 6.3). She met, formally and informally, with most classroom teachers on a monthly basis. In addition, there is ample evidence of formal and informal conversations about reading and writing (as seen in Ms. Matthews's experience) between teachers, librarians, and administrators. Teachers and leaders at Adams talked more often and to a greater variety of people about the language arts routine than they did about the mathematics routine.

EPISTEMOLOGICAL DIFFERENCES AND LEADERSHIP PRACTICE

The leadership practice at Adams reflects epistemological differences in reading, writing, and mathematics. Mathematics is linear and sequential and often concrete, while language arts is a complex web of reading and writing that is not contained in one class subject. Mathematics looks similar across different settings. High school mathematics departments look similar in

Figure 6.2. Mathematics Social Network Connected with the Five-Week Assessment Routine

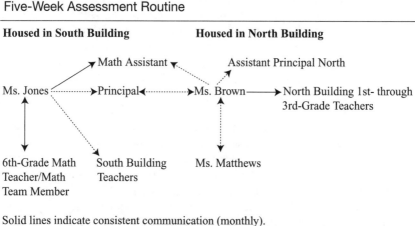

Solid lines indicate consistent communication (monthly).
Dotted lines indicate infrequent communication (several times per year).
Absence of line indicates little to no communication.

Figure 6.3. Language Arts Social Network Connected with the
Five-Week Assessment Routine

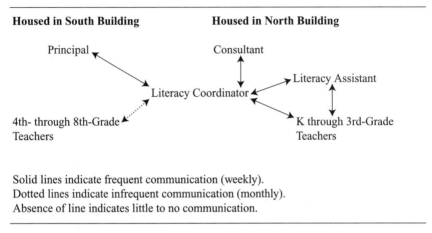

Solid lines indicate frequent communication (weekly).
Dotted lines indicate infrequent communication (monthly).
Absence of line indicates little to no communication.

different districts (Johnson, 1990). Leinhardt and Smith (1985) found that 8
fourth-grade mathematics teachers spontaneously taught fractions the same
way using the same text, teaching lessons on the same topic in approximately
the same order, and using the same pages of text and very similar examples.
One reason for these structural similarities may be that "mathematics is based
on permanent and predictable relationships that can be expressed in principles and rules" (Johnson, 1990, p. 180).

Another explanation for the differences between subject-matter domains
is differences in how people perceive them. Research has shown that math
teachers perceive math as highly structured and sequential (Stodolsky, 1988),
while English is seen as more open and flexible (Stodolsky & Grossman,
1995). Although mathematics is perceived by teachers as linear, there is a
greater variety of cognitive goals in literacy (Ball, 1981; Paule, 1986). Not
everyone agrees that language arts is less linear than mathematics. This perception of mathematics as linear and sequential can be mapped to some strategies for teaching early reading (see Slavin & Madden, 2001, for example).

Mathematics leadership practice at Adams was perceived and enacted
in ways that indicate the preconception that mathematics was linear and
sequential. School leaders provided teachers with a pacing guide and a standardized textbook with which to teach mathematics. They scheduled little
time for teachers to collaborate around mathematics ideas, and they did not
provide time to analyze and discuss assessment data. The infrequent professional development sessions in mathematics most often included math lead-

ers sharing mathematics instructional strategies gleaned from outside experts (Burch & Spillane, 2003).

Leadership practice in reading was different from that in mathematics. As in mathematics, reading instruction was guided by the standardized test, but the ways in which teachers enacted reading instruction were more often left to their individual judgment. Teachers used a variety of curricular materials; had ample meeting time to discuss strategies, ideas, and assessment data; and had a full-time literacy coordinator to support their instructional efforts.

Writing leadership practice at Adams is closer to mathematics practice in terms of how prescribed the leaders made the instructional plan. Like the pacing guide in mathematics, teachers had a timeline for covering the various writing genres. Additionally, leaders and teachers at Adams taught students to write for a standardized testing audience. They built a formula for writing a persuasive, expository, or descriptive essay: five paragraphs (introduction, three paragraphs of body, conclusion), with each paragraph to include a topic sentence and several examples. Leaders at Adams built tools to support writing practice and used their own expertise to support writing instruction rather than depending on external experts; Ms. Tracy and Ms. Kelly both generated writing prompts and consistently assessed and gave feedback on student writing. Additionally, Ms. Kelly handed out writing lessons and assignments, and encouraged teachers to enter writing contests. While the teachers had choice about the content of their writing instruction— they could choose what prompts their students wrote about—they did not have freedom in the structure or the genre of writing they taught. These differences in the definitions of reading, writing, and mathematics are reflected in the ways teachers and school leaders used tools in their practice, as well as their practice itself. Table 6.4 shows a breakdown of leader control over and support for classroom instruction, and leader support for collaborative conditions across mathematics, writing, and reading.

CONCLUSION

In this chapter, I examine one organizational routine at Adams, the Five-Week Assessment routine, in order to develop a better understanding of how leaders build their practice differently in language arts and mathematics. Although the mathematics and language arts Five-Week Assessment routines had similar origins, goals, and ostensive aspects, the routines in practice were very different. Considering aspects of the routine as they relate to a control organization, we see that the designed routines had similar

Table 6.4. Elements of Leadership Control and Support for Mathematics, Writing, and Reading

	Mathematics	**Writing**	**Reading**
Instructional materials	Standardized textbook (No teacher discretion)	Various writing projects (High teacher discretion)	Various textbooks (Medium–high teacher discretion)
Instructional pacing	Pacing guide (No teacher discretion)	Pacing guide (No teacher discretion)	Topic list (Some teacher discretion within each topic)
Leadership tools to support instruction	Homegrown based on external structures (pacing guide based on textbook, assessments pulled from textbook)	Homegrown lesson plans, writing prompts, formula for writing a good essay	Variety of internal and external tools (research, homegrown lesson plans, websites)
Content of in-house professional development and leadership support	Teacher Leader sessions based on external classes Math Team attended	Explicit writing lessons and strategies shared in literacy meetings	Meetings held to share practice and discuss ideas, challenges, and strategies
Five-Week Assessment data analysis and feedback	Scores compiled but not analyzed or shared	Individual support through written feedback on students' writing	Reading scores shared several times throughout the year
Meetings leaders carve out to discuss (on average, per year)	2	2	4
Teacher talk (formal and informal)	Low	Medium	High

inputs and outputs, and both lacked formal and consistent behavior controls. The leaders and teachers used those inputs and outputs differently. In mathematics, the routine enacted was linear and straightforward. Leaders and teachers used input controls in rigid ways, built shallow social networks, and depended on external sources for much of their expertise. Conversely, the input controls in language arts were more open and allowed for teachers to have more discretion in their instructional practices, particularly in reading. The tools leaders built for mathematics reflected externally designed tools. The tools they built for writing were homegrown, and the reading tools were a combination of both external and internal expertise.

There are several possible reasons for the differences in how the Five-Week Assessment routine was enacted in mathematics and language arts at Adams. First, teachers and leaders hold different perceptions about subject matter, which influence their practice. The majority of teachers and leaders believe that teaching mathematics is easier than teaching reading and writing. While epistemological differences do exist between mathematics and language arts, teaching all subjects well is a nonroutine activity, despite these different conceptions of the complexities across language arts and math instruction held by teachers and leaders.

Second, school leadership practice that is focused on improved student performance in math and language arts must have coherence. There was a difference in program coherence in mathematics and language arts at Adams from 2000–2003. The math program had coherence, while the language arts program did not. While largely dependent on the textbook, the Math Team developed a coherent plan for each grade level to cover the concepts tested on the high-stakes tests. The straightforward enactment of the math routine may be a reflection of the straightforward nature of the math program that the Math Team created.

Third, teachers and instructional leaders need a common language. Communities of practice work effectively when they have a joint enterprise and a common language. Math has a common language, both in general and within Adams, but language arts does not. Language arts is a school subject that lies in the intersection of multiple domains (English, speech, communications, literature, etc.). Therefore, it lacks the disciplinary clarity that math possesses. In addition, the wide range of materials that teachers and leaders at Adams used in language arts speaks to the lack of common language within the school as a whole. Adams did not have a common curriculum, and teachers and leaders did not have a common understanding of what their language arts goals were, aside from improving test scores in reading and writing. Implementing a common set of curricular materials is one way for schools to begin to build a common language across their faculty.

These differences have implications for leadership practice. School leaders build and use tools differently in language arts and math. The social networks in these two disciplines reflect epistemological differences. To some extent, these differences also reflect particular attitudes about teaching language arts and math. School leaders need to be supported in examining their assumptions about subject matter—both how math, reading, and writing should be taught (such as what tools and social structures are necessary to support instruction) and how difficult each subject is to teach.

I would like to further examine how subject matter influences leadership practice by examining knowledge, expertise, and teacher beliefs about epistemological differences between math and language arts on a broader scale. While elementary teachers are considered to have less subject-matter expertise in math than in reading and writing, I hypothesize that teachers think they know more about reading but, in fact, may not. Teaching urban students to read, particularly when they are repeating third grade, is not an easy task.

School leaders enact their practice differently in mathematics than they do in language arts. In developing a better understanding of how their practice is enacted, through the examination of an organizational routine, I developed a better understanding of these differences, with the hope of better supporting school leaders in their work to improve teaching and learning.

School Leadership Practice and the School Subject: The Baxter Case

Patricia Burch
UNIVERSITY OF WISCONSIN–MADISON

It is early morning at Baxter Elementary School in Chicago, and teachers have gathered in two separate rooms to talk about instruction as they do every Tuesday. They are participating in two of the many organizational routines designed to lead instructional improvement. In the library, the Literacy Committee is meeting. The room is abuzz as teachers debate what constitutes real literature in a literature-based curriculum. A junior teacher is arguing vehemently against the inclusion of trade books. Down the hall, in Susan Brown's sixth-grade classroom, another group of teachers has gathered, in this case to talk about mathematics instruction. In this room, one teacher, the chair of the committee, does most of the talking. The focus of the meeting is whether or not to purchase a new curriculum. The impetus behind the two meetings is the same—concern over slumping test scores in the middle grades. However, interactions among participants in the mathematics routine have a strikingly different flavor from those of the literacy routine.

In this chapter, I explore the relationship between subject matter and school leadership practice through a case study of Baxter Elementary School. I argue that the leadership practice that developed at Baxter School differed substantially for literacy as compared with mathematics. In particular, teachers sought myriad ways to participate in the organizational routines related to literacy. Literacy coordinators and the principal welcomed and nurtured teacher participation, and teachers were involved in the creation of tools that supported instructional leadership and change. In contrast, in mathematics, one individual—a formally designated teacher leader—primarily set the agenda in mathematics-related routines. Teachers participated in the mathematics-related routines by largely following the agenda established by the teacher leader and did not seek to influence the agenda to the same degree as teachers in the literacy community. Instructional change was supported primarily through the use of externally designed tools (e.g., mathematics curricular materials). These dynamics illuminate how subject matter serves as an important context for school leadership practice.

For close to 2 decades, researchers have documented the importance of subject matter for the work of classroom teachers and teacher leaders (McLaughlin & Talbert, 1993; Siskin, 1991b, 1994; Stodolsky, 1988). High school teachers specialize in particular subject areas and adhere to subcultures linked to these subject areas. Even though most elementary school teachers do not have well-defined, subject-matter specialties, subject matter also appears to be an important context for their practice and efforts to improve their practice (Burch & Spillane, 2003; Spillane, 2005). Although studies have explored the interaction between subject matter and teachers' classroom practice, few have looked at the relationship between subject matter and school leadership at the elementary school level, especially the role of teachers in leadership. To begin to open this black box, I compare how leadership practices for instructional improvement, with the same overarching goal, evolved in different school subjects within one elementary school. I spent 2 school years beginning in 1998 conducting fieldwork at Baxter. During this period, I conducted repeated interviews with three school administrators, twelve classroom teachers, and three curriculum coordinators. I also observed repeated formal and informal organizational routines.[1]

SCHOOL CONTEXT

Baxter Elementary School is located within a racially and ethnically diverse community in Chicago. In the area where the school is located, there are several Jewish synagogues. It is a first-stop community for Russian Jews, newly emigrated to the United States. In addition, the school is adjacent to a vibrant Pakistani and Indian commercial district, which draws many families to the community and school. The school used to have a significant Korean population, but their proportion of the student body is now dwindling. The school serves primarily a low-income population. In the first year of the study, approximately 70% of the students' families qualified for free or reduced-price lunch. Over the past decade, Baxter has built a reputation as a successful school, as reflected in its standardized test scores in reading and mathematics.

In the 1980s, the Chicago school district undertook significant reforms in school governance. The School Reform Act of 1988 dismantled one of the largest central office bureaucracies in the nation and transferred significant authority over instructional matters to the school level. Baxter's current principal, Jim Stern, came to the school at the outset of the decentralization reform with over a decade's experience as principal of an elementary school in a neighboring state.

THE PRINCIPAL'S VISION OF INSTRUCTIONAL IMPROVEMENT AND ENGAGING TEACHERS IN LEADERSHIP PRACTICE

Stern wanted to move the school toward a constructivist approach to teaching and learning in both reading and mathematics—an approach that recognized that students' prior knowledge and understanding was a critical consideration in designing effective instruction. His constructivist vision of instruction reflected themes in national, state, and local reforms of the late 1990s that encouraged teachers to move away from an exclusive focus on drilling, discrete decoding, and computational skills in reading and mathematics. From Stern's perspective, this meant reducing teachers' reliance on textbooks in literacy and encouraging them to use children's literature to foster students' comprehension and writing skills. In mathematics, this meant encouraging teachers to build students' ability to investigate mathematical problems.

Stern also wanted to develop a highly participatory decision-making infrastructure—composed of committees and routines—for leading these improvement efforts in instruction. He described the impetus for the latter as "developing indigenous faculty leadership that is helping our faculty teams become more independent and in developing systems where our joint faculty leadership group plays a much more independent and substantial role in making decisions about how we're going to allocate our curriculum and instructional resources." Stern was intent on building systems of practice for leadership at Baxter that actively involved teachers. In his view, teacher leadership was the primary vehicle for leading instructional change at Baxter.

Stern's original vision was to design a system of practice for leadership that would allow broad-based and systematic input into schoolwide planning for improving instruction. On occasion, Stern used the image of a wheel to describe the leadership structure that he envisioned for Baxter. At the center of the wheel (its axis) was a group that Stern had named "the faculty leadership group." The faculty leadership group was composed of cycle chairs, who were appointed by the principal, as well as key administrators within the school, including the principal, school librarian, school social worker, assistant principal, and dean of student services. The faculty leadership group met monthly.

In addition to the faculty leadership group, Stern convened grade-level cycles that met twice a month. There were three cycles in the school: K–2, 3–5, and 6–8. The vision behind the cycles was to create a structure whereby teachers from adjoining grade groups could meet and plan curriculum together. In this sense, Stern felt that the cycles represented the spokes on Baxter's leadership wheel. Cycle chairs participated on the faculty leadership group. In the context of cycle meetings, chairs provided other members with updates on activities and issues within the faculty leadership group.

One teacher recalled the development of the cycles as a turning point for faculty interaction. "It was the second year after I came. So if I came in '90, I probably became chairperson in '91. That's when we created the cycles. So I was elected the first year we created cycles. . . . Before that, we never met or if we wanted to meet it was on a personal basis." Working with key administrators and teachers, Stern institutionalized a set of organizational routines designed to engage teachers in the work of moving instruction toward a constructivist approach. Reflecting the perspective of several other teachers, the teacher quoted above viewed the creation of cycles as giving faculty their first structured opportunity to talk collectively about classroom instruction and its improvement.

READING AND MATHEMATICS
MOVE TO THE FOREGROUND
ON THE SCHOOLS' IMPROVEMENT AGENDA

In the late 1990s members of the faculty leadership team designed the school's first formally named subject-specific routines: a Literacy Committee and a Mathematics Committee. The principal appointed members to each committee and designated a chair. This decision coincided with district policy developments that placed increasing emphases on improving standardized test scores in reading and mathematics—developments that likely contributed to the decision to make reading and math the focus of leadership efforts at Baxter. Reflecting on that period, Stern referred to standardized test scores as a helpful wake-up call for the school. While Baxter was a high-performing school compared with many in the district in absolute scores, further analysis showed that students' growth was not as impressive when compared with other schools in the area. He commented, "I think we really shook people up quite a bit when we did this test score analysis. It made it clear that out of 12 schools, you know, Baxter was either at the bottom, or very close to the bottom, in terms of the amount of actual growth the kids were making. . . . It was a reality check." As a sign of their concern about test scores in the two content areas, Stern and the faculty leadership group formed the two committees—one to look specifically at issues of reading and the other to concentrate on mathematics. During the time of the study, each committee met twice a month before the official start of school. The principal assigned a chair to each committee to facilitate the routine: the gifted program coordinator for literacy and a sixth-grade science teacher for mathematics. He asked each group to work on increasing the alignment of Baxter's curriculum horizontally (across teachers within a grade level) and vertically (across adjoining grade levels). Stern termed the reform "the 60/40 overlap." The title reflected the premise that while teachers should have some autonomy (40%) in the design of their curriculum, 60% of what they taught should reflect a common curriculum. Stern's hope was that the committees and routines would actively engage teachers in leading instructional improvement and contribute to improvement in student achievement.

THE LITERACY AND MATHEMATICS ORGANIZATIONAL ROUTINES COMPARED

A casual observer might conclude that the practice of leading improvement in mathematics and literacy at Baxter was more alike than different. Teachers' and administrators' talk suggested a school moving aggressively to improve teachers' practice in both content areas. In language arts, leadership efforts focused on creating a literature-rich environment within the school. Teachers received a substantial stipend annually to create their own classroom libraries. Teachers in this group were quite optimistic about Baxter's goal of helping students think more deeply and critically about what they were reading and to help teachers (particularly upper-grade teachers) move toward thinking about literacy as fundamental to learning in any subject. In the context of meetings, teachers would talk about and reflect on differences between more conventional approaches to teaching reading (e.g., basal readers, trade books) and reading organized around students' experiences and authentic texts (e.g., novels). As evidence of his commitment, the principal regularly attended meetings of the Literacy Committee. In 1997, he also secured the funds to hire a full-time program coordinator to work on literacy-related activities schoolwide and within individual classrooms.

Concurrently, school leadership efforts were designed to reform mathematics. The school principal (with the assistance of the sixth-grade science teacher) volunteered to have the school serve as a pilot school for an integrated mathematics and science curriculum developed by a local university. Initially, a select group of teachers participated in training around the curriculum. Eventually, the principal and the Local School Council secured funds to purchase the curriculum and provided interested teachers with preliminary training. In 1999, the school recruited two new teachers with certification in mathematics. In these ways, efforts to lead improvement in literacy and mathematics instruction appeared to move on parallel tracks in terms of routines, resources, and rhetoric. However, over time, substantive differences in the leadership practice in literacy and mathematics routines emerged and became central to my research.

It is within the practice of leadership that ideas and values about learning and tools for learning become evident. In comparing the leadership practices (goals, strategies, interaction patterns, and tools) of literacy-related routines with those identified as critical in mathematics-related routines, it became apparent that subject matter was important in whether and how Baxter teachers engaged in instructional reforms.

In literacy-related leadership routines, classroom teachers contributed ideas and expertise easily and seemingly effortlessly. In Literacy Committee meetings, the hierarchy of new teacher versus veteran teacher, which was quite apparent in cycle meetings, was absent. People ate popcorn, laughed together, shared real-life teaching stories, and, at times, argued collegially. In mathematics-related leadership routines, there were fewer opportunities for teachers to contribute to the work and more emphasis and reliance on formal "sources of expertise" (e.g., prepared curricula and formal training). Mathematics Committee meetings had an undercurrent of nervousness and fear. There was never food, and there was rarely argumentation. There were fewer opportunities for teachers to talk about what *they* were doing in their classrooms but many opportunities to review commercially prepared curricula.

These differences in leadership practice reflect wider views of literacy as having less-defined areas of expertise and of mathematics as a highly defined discipline in which expertise develops outside of the school and through formal training. I explore these patterns below.

LEADERSHIP PRACTICE FOR LITERACY: SEEKING AND RECOGNIZING THE CONTRIBUTIONS OF CLASSROOM TEACHERS

Efforts to lead improvement in literacy at Baxter involved a highly participatory process in which a cross-section of teachers contributed to executing the organizational routines at the core of improvement efforts. In 1993, the Local School Council, a school-based, decision-making body, voted to adopt what it termed a literature-based curriculum. A second-grade teacher, Shirley Woo, was a member of the Literacy Committee. Woo liked the idea of moving away from basal readers in her classroom, but was unclear about what a literature-based curriculum would entail. She purchased a teacher's guide to literature-based curriculum called *Mosaic of Thought*, which helped her understand the difference between learning to read and learning to comprehend. This distinction was important because the school served large numbers of students for whom English was not a first language. Woo worried that while students were mastering the mechanics of reading, their comprehension lagged far behind.

Woo brought the book to the attention of members of the Literacy Committee, who read the book and discussed it during meetings and then decided to make it available to all teachers. Woo recalls:

> At one point Debbie Porter, who was the associate principal a few years back, the two of us went to a bookstore that sold teacher materials, and one of the books that I picked up there was *Mosaic of Thought*, and I brought it back to the committee and I said, "This has been—I mean it really has affected my thinking about reading." As a primary teacher, I focus on helping the children learn to read the words and—and I just automatically assumed that children were able to do things that you tell them to do, like summarize stories or—or use their prior knowledge or whatever else and—and I read this book, and I just felt that we needed to focus more on—on comprehension. So I talked to Debbie and Tina [the curriculum coordinator] about the book. They picked up on it, and as the Literacy Committee, we decided it would be a good idea to introduce the book to the whole faculty.

These events reflect a larger pattern in leadership practice for literacy. At Baxter, formally designed arrangements for leadership—routines, leadership positions—were important, as reflected in the Literacy Committee meetings and curriculum coordinator position. But informal leaders like Woo were also critical. Woo, who had no formally designated leadership position, influenced the direction of literacy reform efforts through her active participation in the Literacy Committee routine. Further, formally designated leaders at Baxter took her idea seriously and adopted it as part of their efforts to lead improvement in literacy instruction. This sharing of leadership was common; Woo was not an exception at Baxter.

Over the next several years, through the Literacy Committee routine and other related organizational routines, teachers cultivated and assumed a wide variety of leadership roles in efforts to improve literacy instruction. Two teachers sought ways of helping teachers build classroom libraries stocked with children's literature. With the librarian, they wrote a successful grant that provided each teacher with annual funds to purchase books. The Literacy Committee also organized an annual read-a-thon that challenged students to read more books. When they met the challenge, the principal stood on the roof of the school building and read excerpts from his favorite children's literature. A second-grade teacher started a parent–child book club and after-school program focused on literacy. A fifth-grade teacher collaborated with the literacy coordinator to prepare students for a citywide writing competition. Over time, a cross-section of teachers moved in and out of leadership roles for literacy instruction depending on the routine or task at hand. Sometimes these informal leaders worked with formally designated leaders (e.g., curriculum coordinator, librarian), but often they worked alone or with their teacher colleagues. Working under the umbrella of the Literacy Committee, they designed new organizational routines for leading improvement in literacy (parent–child book club, annual read-a-thon).

With the help of other teachers on the Literacy Committee, Woo organized a monthly reading group for teachers. The literacy coordinator described the meetings as giving teachers a forum for discussing literacy instruction, where "before it was just everybody close the door." She also viewed this organizational routine as helping teachers develop a common language to talk about what they were doing. She recalls:

> This book, *Mosaic of Thought*, was purchased for every single faculty member, and I know not everybody read it, but we did do some discussion groups within our, you know, grade level, cycle meetings, and stuff. And we did do, you know, a few activities and things around the book. Not as much as we probably should have, but most of the people read the book and most of the people started using some of the common vocabulary that came from it, and, you know, I think it moved us forward.

Mosaic of Thought became an important tool in different organizational routines —grade-level meetings, cycle meetings, Literacy Committee meetings. Two members of the Literacy Committee separately referred to the book as the school's "bible." It helped focus discussions on literacy instruction and enabled school leaders and teachers to develop a common vocabulary for talking about the work of instructional improvement.

As teachers and school leaders interacted over time on shared problems using a common set of tools, they negotiated differences and developed shared meanings about the work of leading improvement in literacy instruction. The Literacy Committee routine served as an umbrella routine in that all other routines were vetted, tweaked, and approved in the Literacy Committee. One issue that emerged as a central point of discussion was the fact that many teachers were still struggling with how to translate general principles and strategies of a literature-based curriculum into actual classroom practices. The meetings of the Literacy Committee became a setting for discussing these issues. Over time, members of the Literacy Committee determined that their fellow classroom teachers needed concrete ideas to bring the literacy reform *into* their classrooms.

In response to this challenge, several teachers with no formal leadership designations proposed and organized a one-day inservice. They organized the inservice around classroom strategies associated with a literature-based approach, such as writers' workshop—a strategy that was highlighted in *Mosaic of Thought*. Rather than hiring an outsider, the inservice designers invited Baxter teachers who felt comfortable with writers' workshop to lead the staff development. A teacher involved in the development recalled, "We gathered together some faculty that might want to share with the rest of the faculty just some things that they've done in their classroom that—that teach these strategies that *Mosaic of Thought* identifies as being what we called the core propositions." She characterized presenters as a "real varied group" both in terms of grade levels and levels of experience. After the inservice, several teachers identified the session as an important event for the school because it helped teachers see the practices outlined in the book through real-life examples modeled by fellow Baxter teachers. A version of the inservice was offered the following year, this time focusing on word walls.

Thus, in literacy, the establishment of a decision-making structure devoted to literacy issues provided a setting for the creation of other literacy-related routines, including book fairs and school-based inservices. Both formally designated leaders and informal leaders were active in the establishment of these routines. For example, the principal helped persuade the Local School Council to secure the money to purchase *Mosaic of Thought*. He also negotiated with district administrators for a waiver that allowed the school to organize its own staff development in reading rather than having faculty participate in a district-led workshop focused on the district's new reading curriculum. The school principal and other formally designated leaders expected, encouraged, and created opportunities for teachers to take on leadership roles for literacy instruction (e.g., by leading workshops, suggesting topics for meetings, and analyzing data). The two literacy coordinators rotated responsibility for chairing the committee for several years. One literacy coordinator then mentored a fifth- and sixth-grade teacher to take over the chair position, and that teacher assumed the role of chair with primary responsibility for the Literacy Committee routine. When teachers proposed new organizational routines to lead improvement in literacy, formally designated leaders helped and encouraged them.

By several teachers' reports, the distribution of expertise over both formally designated leaders and informal leaders in literacy contributed to a climate whereby even new teachers (to the school or to the committee) perceived themselves as actively contributing to Baxter's literacy reforms. For example, a first-year teacher recalled being pleasantly surprised by her welcome from other Literacy Committee members: "I kind of walked in there, and I felt kind of—because it was my first time in a literacy meeting and I felt like I was budging in, but they were really nice." Recalling these events, the literacy coordinator further described the climate within literacy meetings:

> And then Susan Cielo, who is a third-grade teacher this year, she's a relatively new teacher. And she comes to the committee more with very thoughtful concerns than solutions. But that's really nice to have that voice on the committee. I mean she really . . . spends a lot of time sort of analyzing her own teaching and the dynamics of her particular cycle and some of the difficulties that are going on there around literacy instruction and really clearly articulates them and doesn't let things go. So she's been a real helpful force on the committee too.

The expertise for the execution of the Literacy Committee routine, then, was distributed over both formally designated leaders and informal leaders.

LEADERSHIP PRACTICE FOR LITERACY: GENERATING TOOLS IN-HOUSE

The Literacy Committee developed a number of new tools for leading improvement in literacy instruction inside the school. In addition to the teacher talk sessions noted above, literacy leaders engaged in diagnostic work about instruction by developing a needs assessment that surveyed teachers on their reactions to literacy reforms. Members of the Literacy Committee developed the three-page survey. One teacher recalled,

> We did a survey of the faculty to find out kind of where we stood. And this was probably 4 years ago. And what we discovered was that the teachers, after about second or third grade, didn't think of themselves as teachers of reading at all. It was like they teach that in first or second grade, and now I'm teaching my subject, my content area.

This teacher then described how the team used survey results: "So, as we kind of, as we looked at the survey that we gave to everybody, we saw the pattern emerging that people didn't consider themselves teachers of reading and they didn't know—didn't have a clue on where to begin teaching reading. So we, that was kind of the beginning, our realization that that was a problem area." Literacy leaders identified the school as capable of generating its own tools to build its knowledge base in literacy, rather than relying on tools developed externally.

Literacy leaders also developed two new rubrics. One was a new system for assessing teachers' efforts with practices such as writers' workshop. The curriculum coordinator floated the idea of a rubric with select teachers, and together they developed several rubrics. She recalled, "At the beginning of the year, we focused on writing and developing assessments to work with the kids on their writing, with rubrics that the kids would see ahead of time so that we were not surprising them with some sort of random assessment at the end of all their work." She further explained, "Well, it broke it down—those ideas it broke down, but then we developed rubrics and so the rubrics then—what we did was we came up with questions that the kids could sort of ask of one another and of themselves under each heading. You know and ideas and organization. And it would be tailored to the project, but they would all, you know, so whatever it was they were writing that the rubrics might alter slightly, although there would always be those—those major headings." Her colleague developed another rubric aimed at helping teachers select children's literature. In these and other accounts, literacy leaders articulated a need to create tools in-house to work on literacy reforms. In order to adequately assess their efforts, they developed another rubric, tailored to their current efforts to lead improvement in literacy instruction.

Thus, for Baxter's administrators and teachers, leadership for literacy was stretched over formally designated leaders and classroom teachers with different interests and levels of experience. Not all classroom teachers took on responsibility for leadership practice. Moreover, those who took responsibility for leadership practice differed depending on the particular organizational routine. Classroom teachers also played a critical role in identifying and introducing some of the key tools that enabled leadership practice for literacy at Baxter, such as *Mosaics of Thought*. Finally, classroom teachers' leadership responsibilities were not confined to executing the leadership routines designed by formally designated leaders; some classroom teachers proposed and designed some of the key routines for leading improvement in literacy at Baxter.

MATHEMATICS COMMUNITY: RELYING ON ONE LEADER

Leadership for mathematics at Baxter differed from leadership for literacy. Responsibility for leadership routines related to mathematics was distributed across fewer individuals, with one formally designated leader, Mrs. Brown, who had a graduate degree in mathematics and science, taking most of the responsibility for executing key organizational routines—including serving as the chair of the committee. Other members of the Mathematics Committee included a teacher who had taught upper-grade math for 8 years and a teacher who had participated in a training workshop for integrating mathematics, science, and technology.

In comparison to literacy, there were fewer opportunities for regular classroom teachers to participate in leading mathematics reforms. One individual, rather than several as in the case of literacy, chaired the committee over the course of 2 years. During meetings, Brown always sat at the head of the table. She also set the agenda for the meeting and rarely solicited any input from other committee members about the content of that agenda. In addition, in the context of meetings, there was simply less "discussion." Brown would provide updates about conferences that she had attended or materials that she had read. On occasion, a teacher might ask a clarifying question. However, there was very rarely any discussion that probed or debated the committee's direction. To illuminate this, I offer the following field notes of a November 1999 Mathematics Committee meeting:

> This morning, as on other mornings, the committee meets in Brown's room. The purpose of the meeting, as Brown explained to the group, is to create a set of guidelines for teachers in the 7th and 8th grades to use in developing mathematics units. This task is part of the curricular alignment agenda proposed by the principal. "Do you think it is possible for us to create these guidelines?" Brown asks. A few teachers nod their heads. Brown then proposes that they start by reviewing the guidelines developed by the district in mathematics and science and then adapt them. More head nodding and then silence. Finally, one teacher tells Brown her plan sounds like a good one. In response, Brown hands out photocopies of the district standards that she has made. She passes the copies around, and teachers begin to read them. One teacher asks for clarification of the term "hands-on mathematics," and Brown responds quickly, referring to the district standards in her hand to support her definition.

Following this meeting, a teacher characterized this set of interactions as "fairly typical." In contrast to organizational routines related to literacy, in mathematics there was little discussion about how new curricular ideas were being enacted in classrooms and little in-depth discussion to define somewhat vague terms like "hands-on mathematics" or how people's understandings of these terms could vary from one classroom to the next. Meeting routines were only one of many sources of difference between leadership practice in mathematics compared with leadership practice in literacy. In mathematics, there were simply fewer mathematics-related routines. There was a poorly attended math fair that involved parents, but little evidence of other schoolwide mathematics routines (e.g., school-based math inservice activities).

One distinguishing characteristic of leadership for mathematics instruction at Baxter was that one person, Brown, did most of the work. She was the primary mover-and-shaker in executing the Mathematics Committee routine. With an undergraduate degree in mathematics, Brown was the exclusive author of grant proposals to extend math reforms to upper grades. Recall that in literacy, teachers worked together on numerous occasions to select and discuss curricular materials, design new tools for student assessment, and make presentations about their work. In contrast, the practice in organizational routines related to mathematics looked very different—in particular, the exchange of predeveloped, externally generated ideas.

The chair and chief mover-and-shaker in the Mathematics Committee routine also served as the school's main contact with external resources. At one faculty meeting, Brown sat at the back of the auditorium. When the time came to recognize faculty contributions in literacy, the principal identified eight teachers as making important contributions in efforts to lead improvement in literacy. Once his list was exhausted, several teachers in the audience called out the names of other teachers they felt should be recognized. The dynamic for the mathematics awards was entirely different. The principal asked only Brown to stand up. He credited her alone with the development of a successful request for proposal and commended her for her role as committee chair. Later, the principal described Brown's role in the community in this way:

> There is a lot of excitement within that group [Mathematics Committee] about taking some of the work that [Brown's] been involved in and getting the stuff that would allow us to dole it out to more people. [Brown's] been so actively involved in the development of that stuff as well as the implementation of it. She, of course, has a very strong mathematics and science background and got an inside track and gets all sorts of good stuff for us.

In these comments, the principal identified Brown as the school's in-house expert and leader for mathematics instruction. He defined her expertise chiefly in terms of her formal credentials rather than her classroom or practical experience. Teachers also characterized Brown as leading improvement efforts in mathematics instruction at Baxter. One stated, "[Brown] is working very hard on trying to get us organized and get focused and get us going somewhere. We have no focus at this point. We have no direction." This teacher, speaking for the group, viewed herself as relying on Brown's leadership skills and connections to the field. In this way, regular classroom teachers involved in the Mathematics Committee routine contributed to defining leadership practice for mathematics instruction at Baxter. By virtue of their willingness to sit back and let Brown take over the show, leadership practice for mathematics looked different from leadership practice for literacy.

The principal characterized regular classroom teachers as following Brown's lead. Brown had the contacts and will to make the connections to both professional developers and university partners. Regular classroom teachers were yet to be identified as leaders in the work of improving mathematics instruction at Baxter. Echoing this view, Brown similarly characterized other teachers who participated in the Mathematics Committee meetings as novices in terms of their expertise. She said, "So we're really at the point where they're still trying to figure out, 'Well, what do I need?' Not really at the depth of, 'So, how am I teaching this?' or, 'What am I throwing out, and what am I not throwing out?'" In contrast to the literacy chairs who viewed novice teachers as playing important leadership roles, Brown defined herself as the lone expert and leader for efforts to improve mathematics instruction that she believed were still in their infancy.

MATHEMATICS COMMUNITY: RELYING MORE ON EXTERNAL TOOLS

The tools sought out by mathematics and literacy leaders were distinctly different. Reflecting a view of mathematics expertise as defined by credentials and formal training, the mathematics leaders and indeed teachers relied heavily on externally developed tools for most of their work. A university-based curriculum known as TIMS was mentioned most frequently. Mathematics and science professors at a local university developed TIMS, which targets students in fifth and sixth grades. Hence, while there were a lot of resources available to Baxter teachers as they worked on mathematics instruction, few of them were developed inside the school. Reflecting broader subject-matter norms regarding the importance of external expertise, the tools were developed by outside experts. Further reflecting this perspective, Brown identified the TIMS curriculum as the primary engine for improving instruction: "When I came into Baxter, TIMS was kind of already on its way. It had just started. Seeds were planted in lower grades. So it's helped with the upper-grade discussions a lot because that momentum was already there. So when we had a standards-based curriculum in our primary grades, it was very easy to convince the upper-grade teachers that that's something that we should be doing. It's not—it wasn't a question. I like TIMS a lot as a curriculum. It's proven, to us—I mean data don't lie." In mathematics, the end-goal, as framed by Brown, was broad-based buy-in and support for curriculum that outside experts had developed and that had "proven evidence" that it worked.

The principal also shared this emphasis on the importance of external expertise in mathematics reforms. Identifying the TIMS curriculum as a defining characteristic of Baxter's mathematics reforms, Stern stated, "The difference here [between math and literacy] is that there were two missing components for literacy that we had to work with in math. One, we had a very well-articulated scope and sequence curriculum that we could lean on. In addition to that, we had a tremendous amount of staff development support." As reflected in the principal's comments and others' accounts, Baxter's leaders viewed externally developed curriculum and associated staff development as the engine for improving mathematics instruction. In contrast to literacy, they looked primarily outside the school for tools for leading improvement in mathematics instruction.

In summary, from a distributed perspective, tools are not incidental to leadership practice. They are a defining element of that practice. The tools that school leaders, both formally designated leaders and informal leaders, mobilized in their efforts to lead improvement in instruction in each subject area differed between literacy and mathematics. Over the course of the study, the Literacy Committee created several new tools to facilitate its efforts to lead improvement in literacy instruction, including a teacher survey, new student assessments, rubrics for selecting children's literature, reading groups, and so forth. In contrast, the Mathematics Committee relied on externally developed tools as the focal point of its work.

CONCLUSION

Arrangements for leading instruction at Baxter differed depending on the school subject. These differences were reflected in who took responsibility for designing and executing organizational routines and the extent to which these leaders were formally designated or informal leaders. Further, these differences were reflected in the tools that school leaders used in the work and their thinking about the work. Rather than merely the target of school leadership practice, subject matter is an integral element of *how* leadership for literacy and math takes shape. At Baxter, two distinct patterns emerged in leadership practice. First, a cross-section of teachers with no formal leadership designations assumed leadership for literacy reforms. They also designed and led efforts to improve literacy instruction and enlist the support of classroom teachers. In contrast, in mathematics a sole formally designated leader took on most of the responsibility for executing organizational routines. While classroom teachers participated in these routines and brought considerable expertise and resources to the table, they mostly played secondary roles. Furthermore, formally designated leaders played different roles vis-à-vis teachers depending on the school subject. Literacy coordinators worked alongside classroom teachers to lead improvement in literacy instruction. In contrast, the Mathematics Committee chair assumed a more directive role and received most of the credit for leading improvement efforts in mathematics.

A second difference between leadership for mathematics and literacy was the tools that were used in practice. In literacy, both school-designed tools and externally produced tools were used. Indeed, leaders in literacy viewed the creation of tools as a critical component of their work. When they had a question or a need, they designed a survey, rubric, or discussion group in response. In mathematics, leaders relied chiefly on externally developed tools. For example, the adoption of a mathematics curriculum was viewed as the primary engine and focus of their work. The fact that the mathematics curriculum became the focus of leadership practice had significant implications for how leadership practice evolved (or failed to evolve) in that subject. The mathematics curriculum came with consultants. It came with staff development and a highly sequenced set of units for skill development. By its very nature, the curriculum provided fewer opportunities for teachers to contribute to the design of reforms.

While commercially produced external tools such as books and other materials featured in leadership practice related to literacy, they did not feature nearly as prominently as in mathematics. Further, tools developed in-house featured very prominently in leadership practice related to literacy instruction. Baxter did not adopt a new curriculum as part of its effort to lead improvement in literacy instruction. The district recently had developed a literature-based approach to teaching reading and writing that it offered to schools free of charge. Instead, school leaders at Baxter opted to design their own curriculum. They created classroom libraries and encouraged teachers to adopt and adapt practices from a range of resources.

The role of the principal in leadership practice also differed depending on the school subject. First, the principal self-identified and was identified by others as a key leader for literacy instruction. As part of this work, he made varied contributions—some of which are not typically associated with the principal's role. For example, he regularly participated in organizational routines for literacy and contributed agenda items. He designed and implemented an organizational routine, the read-a-thon, to lead improvement in literacy, and he demonstrated his love of literature by reading to children and parents in a culminating celebration. Through these roles, the principal modeled a vision of leadership practice in which leadership for improving literacy was distributed across formal and informal leaders.

The principal's participation in mathematics routines was very different. He rarely participated in the Mathematics Committee. Instead, he communicated with participants via the chair. The principal's actions signaled that leadership for mathematics reforms resided primarily with the chair.

The Baxter case suggests the need to look carefully at the relationship between subject matter and the leadership practice that teachers encounter in schools. School administrators' and teachers' views about subject matter influence how they think about the work of leading improvement in instruction. Subject-matter views are reflected not only in teachers' classroom practices but also in leadership practice. The Baxter case suggests that the routines developed at the suborganizational level of the school—for example, in the context of Literacy and Mathematics Committees—serve as important carriers for broader subject-matter norms. Understanding relations between leadership practice and classroom practice requires close investigation of the values and beliefs enacted in these routines and their relationship to more localized (e.g., school-level) reform goals.

We also need to look more at the interplay between the leadership tools and school leaders' views of subject matter. School leaders select many of the tools that they use in leadership practice. The choices that schools make are critical in that these tools frame and focus the interactions among leaders and between leaders and followers. An emphasis on internally developed tools can create new leadership opportunities for those with no formal leadership designations. Of course, it also can create a lot of work for teachers. For example, at Baxter, teacher talk groups generated a demand for a survey. The survey pointed to the need for more staff development. The more teachers participated in leadership work, the more their ideas and needs came to the fore, leading to more opportunities for teachers to participate in leadership practice.

Alternatively, an emphasis on external tools may have hidden costs in schools' efforts to strengthen teaching practice. At Baxter, the Mathematics Committee relied heavily on an externally developed curriculum. There was less to be done and therefore perhaps fewer opportunities, particularly in comparison to literacy, for nascent leaders to emerge and contribute. At the same time, having outside experts and well-developed curriculum can alleviate workload pressures and give teachers the opportunity to assume other important leadership functions.

A Distributed Perspective
On and *In* Practice

James P. Spillane
NORTHWESTERN UNIVERSITY

John B. Diamond
HARVARD UNIVERSITY

Taking a distributed perspective to investigate school leadership and management, the six cases in this volume challenge some popular usages of the distributed perspective, illustrate the value of taking a distributed perspective, and identify challenges for those working within this perspective. In this final chapter, we examine some crosscutting themes that the cases foreground, focusing on three issues. First, we use examples from the cases to consider the entailments of taking a distributed perspective to understand school leadership and management. What exactly does it mean to take a distributed perspective on school leadership? In doing so, we acknowledge that many scholars and practitioners use the term *distributed leadership* and that there is considerable diversity with respect to what the term means across users. Indeed, we use the term *distributed perspective on leadership and management* intentionally. Our aim here it to make clear what we, as one group of researchers, mean when we take a distributed perspective to study school leadership and management. We are presenting *our perspective* on this construct. Second, using the cases, we consider the utility of a distributed perspective, examining what this perspective helps to uncover about school leadership and management—what value does this perspective add? Third, we consider some challenges for those working to understand leadership and management using a distributed perspective.

TAKING A DISTRIBUTED PERSPECTIVE: GETTING SOME CLARITY ON THE ENTAILMENTS

Clarity about language and constructs is critical for both researchers and practitioners, but it is not easily achieved. It is easier for us to move along using the same terminology to denote different phenomena than to struggle with the hard work of arriving at some "taken as shared" understanding of the terms and constructs we use (Cobb, McClain, & Gravemeijer, 2001). New words, new perspectives, and new approaches enter the education field at a rapid pace, especially with respect to school leadership and management. The school leadership and management bazaar is replete with offerings. This is the nature of the enterprise. Because terminology and approaches come and go at a rapid pace, researchers and practitioners develop a healthy skepticism often summed up by the phrase "this too shall pass." More important, people often make sense of the deluge of terms and constructs by fitting them into existing knowledge structures and never fundamentally changing their understanding. In this way, a distributed perspective simply becomes another term for team leadership or even democratic leadership. Our goal is not to add to an already-crowded bazaar. Instead, clarity with respect to what we mean by a distributed perspective is central.

From a research perspective, clarity is critical because, absent some shared understanding of what it means to take a distributed perspective to the study of school leadership and management, it is difficult to compare findings from different studies claiming to take such a perspective. If scholars use the same terminology to mean different things, then it is impossible for the field to amass a knowledge base, test hypotheses, replicate studies, and move forward. From a practitioner perspective, loose terminology serves only to frustrate improvement efforts as teachers and administrators use the same words to mean different things and talk past one another in their efforts to improve schools. Defining what we mean and working to arrive at some shared understandings of ideas like distributed leadership (the same holds for professional learning communities, instructional leadership, and so on) is critical if these conceptual tools are to be helpful to us in our efforts to understand and reform school leadership and management.

A distributed perspective, like a host of other leadership perspectives, is little more than an analytical or conceptual tool that, depending on how it is used, is more or less helpful to researchers and practitioners in doing their work. What is critical is not having the one best airtight definition, but rather having a working definition that those who use the tool share so that we can have productive conversations about our work. The cases in this volume help define what we mean and don't mean by taking a distributed perspective on school leadership and management and in the process enable us to distinguish our usage from some of the common usages in the field.

CONCEPTUAL LENS AND DIAGNOSTIC TOOL

As is evident from the cases, a distributed perspective on leadership is a conceptual lens or diagnostic frame for examining leadership and management in schools. More specifically, our work was motivated by a desire to develop a conceptual or analytical tool that researchers and practitioners could use to frame their probing of school leadership and management and to examine the implications of their work for classroom instruction and its improvement. As a result, a distributed perspective offers no simple blueprint for how to lead or manage the schoolhouse. Instead, it offers a conceptual or diagnostic tool for researchers and practitioners working on school leadership and management. None of the cases offers a five- or six-step program for others to follow. Instead they take a distributed perspective to understanding practice in five different schools. We are not convinced that such a five- or six-step program exists. Hence, a distributed perspective is descriptive before it is prescriptive (Spillane, 2006). It frames our efforts, as practitioners and researchers, to examine the phenomena of leadership and management and offers some pointers for how we might move forward. In this way, a distributed perspective on leadership offers no simple panacea; it puts the onus on users to diagnose and design school practice well in order to enable improvement.

Because a distributed perspective is not a model but a conceptual lens or diagnostic tool for probing and analyzing practice, some may wonder what this tool contributes to practice. The perspective helps researchers and practitioners make sense of leadership and management practice without prescribing steps for how one *should* lead or manage. Further, over time the empirical research base will do three things. First, theory-building work will continue to help refine the analytical tools that can be used both in the study and development of school leadership and management. Second, a distributed perspective does offer design principles that can be used to guide the work of leading and managing and attempts to develop and improve that work. Third, as the empirical knowledge base develops over time, it will provide school leaders with information about leading and managing practice and its relations with instruction that they can use to inform their work. As the cases in this volume illustrate, taking a distributed perspective to investigate leading and managing the schoolhouse foregrounds the connection to instructional practice. Moreover, it provides a framework for identifying the multiple ways in which leadership and management practice connect to and influence instructional practice.

Some might read our attempts to define what is meant and not meant by a distributed perspective as somewhat presumptuous, but we strive for a catholic dialogue. In seeking clarity about what we mean by a distributed perspective on school leadership and management, we are not striving for some canonical definition. However, we do intend to make our meaning clear, based on our theory-building work over the past 9 years. We acknowledge that our understanding has evolved, and we expect it will evolve more as we move forward. That is the nature of theory-building work. Two examples are illustrative. We started out focusing chiefly on leadership using a working definition that reflected our reading of the literature and our focus on the technical core of schools—teaching and learning. As our work developed, back and forth between theory and empirical data, our definition of leadership evolved (Spillane, 2006). Further, we became increasingly convinced that, while leadership and management may be analytically distinguishable, in practice it was often difficult to distinguish between the two. Specifically, organizational routines that serve leadership functions often serve management functions as well. In practice, leading and maintaining often work in tandem, part and parcel of the same organizational routine. We return to this issue below. This is the nature of theory-building work. And we make no apologies for changing our minds as we strive to redefine what it means to take a distributed perspective based on our research. Our only challenge to readers is to be clear about what they mean when they take up the notion of a distributed perspective and use it in their work as practitioners and researchers.

We also acknowledge that others use the term *distributed leadership* or *a distributed perspective* to mean something different than we do.

So one thing the cases in this volume dispel is that a distributed perspective offers some panacea for improving schools. It is a conceptual or diagnostic tool, used well or not so well, depending on the hands that use it. It is a tool that we anticipate will become better defined over the next several years as we, and others, use it to understand school leadership and management.

DISPELLING THE MYTHS
ABOUT DISTRIBUTED LEADERSHIP

There are several myths about the distributed leadership perspective that the cases in this volume dispel.

Myth #1: The Distributed Perspective Is a Blueprint for Leadership and Management

The distributed perspective often is talked about as though it was an approach to leadership. The cases in this volume suggest that while school leaders intentionally can distribute responsibility for the work of leading and managing the school, it is not a five-step plan for leaders to follow.

As the Adams cases illustrate, if teachers are to develop as leaders, it does not simply happen by decree. Instead, they need opportunities to develop as leaders, and this often involves considerable work on the part of formally designated leaders such as the school principal. As demonstrated in the Halverson analysis of Adams School, leaders created opportunities such as the Breakfast Club organizational routine for teachers to cultivate their leadership capacity, build professional community, and gain the respect of their colleagues. The emergence of teachers as leaders at Adams (particularly around literacy instruction) was in great part a function of the school leaders' efforts. Moreover, teachers need routines within which they can develop as leaders and practice their wares as leaders and managers. Of course, as the Costen case illuminates, teachers can emerge as leaders for school staff even absent the designs and desires of formally designated leaders. In some cases, such teachers move their colleagues in directions that are contrary to those intended by the formally designated school leaders. As the Costen case demonstrated, formally designated leaders ignore such efforts at their peril. Hence, understanding school leadership and management necessitates attention to both the designed organization and the lived organization.

Myth #2: The Distributed Perspective Negates the Role of Principals

A second myth about taking a distributed perspective to examine school leadership and management dispelled by the cases in this volume is that a distributed perspective somehow negates or undermines the role of the head teacher or school principal. It is striking that in the six cases in this volume, all studied from a distributed perspective, the school principal or head teacher looms large. While the school principal plays an important role in each case, his or her prominence differs depending on the leadership function and the school context. While the cases acknowledge the central role of the school principal, they also capture the important role that other formal and informal leaders play in defining the practice of leadership and management. Further, both Burch's and Coldren's chapters illustrate how followers are critical in defining the day-to-day practice of leading and managing schools.

Still, acknowledging the part played by others, including those in followership roles, does not necessitate abandoning the school principal when taking a distributed perspective in research and development efforts.

As the cases illuminate, formally designated leaders are critical, and understanding their work fits easily within a distributed perspective. Moreover, several cases in this book illuminate how heroes and heroines still figure in the work of leadership and management (although they do not figure alone). Chapter 2 emphasized the heroic efforts of Hillside's principal, Barbara Nelson, who reads and gives feedback on students' work and teachers' lesson plans in a school with well over 1,000 students. Accomplishing these leadership tasks while simultaneously attending to the numerous management activities demanded of her is a mind-boggling amount of work. Likewise, Therese Williams's work to transform Adams School partially fits into this model of the heroic leader who turns a troubled institution around. These accounts should dispel any idea that the school principal is somehow rendered less relevant when taking a distributed perspective to understanding school leadership and management. While a distributed perspective acknowledges the importance of multiple leaders, it in no way negates the critical role of the CEO.

Myth #3: From a Distributed Perspective, Everyone Is a Leader

Another myth that the cases dispel is that everyone in a school is a leader when the work is viewed from a distributed perspective. While the distributed perspective focuses our attention on the possibility that anyone in the school, even those with no formally designated leadership positions, could be engaged in the work of leading and managing, it does not assume that everyone is or even should be a leader. These cases dispel this idea by illuminating that not everyone is engaged in the work of leading and managing the schoolhouse. The number of staff involved in leading an organizational routine differed depending on the school, the particular leadership routine, and the subject matter. At Kelly School, there were fewer formally designated leaders than at Adams. This meant that the practice of leadership took a different form in these two contexts. Likewise, Chapters 6 and 7 show how more leaders emerge around literacy instruction than around mathematics instruction. A distributed perspective allows for everyone, even students, to take a lead in the work of leading and managing the school, but does not begin with the assumption that everyone does. At the same time, the distributed perspective does acknowledge that followers are critical in understanding the practice of leading and managing as one of its core constituting elements. But such an acknowledgment does not cast everyone in the role of leader or manager.

We suspect that increasing the number of individuals involved in leading a particular organizational routine may have diminishing returns beyond a certain number—too many cooks may indeed spoil the broth. This, of course, is an empirical question, the answer to which is likely to vary depending on the particular routine: What is the optimal number of leaders? Moreover, an exclusive focus on the number of leaders or on making everyone a leader misses the core issue—it is not the number of individuals but what they contribute to the task and especially how the expertise for carrying out the task is distributed among them. Hence, if one person has the expertise to perform a particular routine effectively, involving five individuals may be a waste of valuable human resources.

Myth #4: Distributed Leadership Is Only About Collaborative Situations

Another myth that these cases dispel is that a distributed perspective implies that leaders are pulling together toward a shared goal; or that it implies agreement and collegial arrangements among those doing the leading and managing. As the Costen case illustrates, a distributed perspective is as relevant in understanding leadership and management in situations where leaders are working for different or even opposing ends as it is in situations where leaders are working toward common ends. School leaders don't have to see eye-to-eye or even get along with one another to work together on leading and managing the schoolhouse; in fact, in some cases their conflicts limit what can be accomplished. The Costen case, where teachers with no formal leadership designations took on leadership roles, illustrates how this can happen in schools despite the desires and designs of those in formally designated leadership positions. In short, a distributed perspective applies to situations where leaders have different or contrary goals as easily as it does to situations where leaders are striving for the same goal.

THE VALUE-ADDED ISSUE

A key question for any analytical or conceptual tool is whether it adds value in practice by enabling researchers to generate new knowledge about a phenomenon and/or helping practitioners to do their work more effectively. The cases in this volume help identify a number of ways in which a distributed perspective adds value to research on school leadership and management. In this section, we consider six ways in which these cases contribute to our understanding of school leadership and management. First, the cases in this volume illustrate how leadership and management play out in tandem in practice. Second, these cases help us understand the *practice* of leading and managing. Third, the cases help us reframe our understanding of the relations between leaders and followers. Fourth, they help illustrate how the situation is an integral, constituting element of leadership and management. Fifth, the cases illustrate how a distributed perspective brings attention to the designed and lived/formal and informal organization. Sixth, they provide clues as to how leadership practice connects to instructional improvement.

LEADING AND MANAGING IN TANDEM

We began our study focusing chiefly on leadership practice, although mindful of Larry Cuban's observation that good management was essential for good leadership. Scholars distinguish between management and leadership (Burns, 1978; Cuban, 1988). Management practice centers on maintaining current ways of doing school business; maintaining the smooth running of a school is paramount. Leadership practice typically focuses on initiating change in the current ways of doing business.

The managerial imperative dominates the work of the school principal (Cuban, 1988). At the same time, the leadership imperative appears to dominate much of what scholars write about leading and managing schools. In the day-to-day work of schools, leading and maintaining often work in tandem, part and parcel of the same organizational routine, and distinguishing between the two can be difficult.

The cases in this volume suggest that distinguishing between organizational routines in terms of maintaining and leading may be difficult in the daily practice of the schoolhouse. In the cases, many of the examples from practice involve both efforts to lead change in business as usual and, in the same routine, attempts to maintain the status quo. Sometimes this happens because different leaders pursue different goals or agendas. Take the Costen case. Principal Kox and her newly appointed assistant principal worked to lead change in business as usual at the school. New organizational routines were designed and implemented. In co-performing organizational routines, Principal Kox and her assistant principal worked to define student achievement as a problem at Costen, arguing that while the school did well relative to other schools in the district, close to half the students were not reading at grade level. Problem definition is a key element of leadership practice. But others, some veteran teachers, worked to maintain the status quo and protect how business was done at Costen, and they did so publicly in many of the same organizational routines that Principal Kox used to lead change. Their attempts did not go unnoticed by many staff members; they exercised influence. At one level, the efforts of these veteran teachers can be viewed as maintenance—an attempt to maintain existing routines. Of course, viewed from another perspective the efforts of these veteran teachers might be defined as leadership practice—an attempt to preserve existing practice in the face of pressure for change. The Costen case points out the complexity of distinguishing management from leadership in the day-to-day practice of the schoolhouse.

But even the same leaders can pursue both management and leadership in the same organizational routine. They can work to maintain some aspects of how business gets done in the organization, while working in tandem to transform other aspects. As the Adams cases illustrate, routines such as the Five-Week Assessment and Literacy Committee meetings included efforts to maintain (e.g., focusing classroom teaching on standards) and lead (e.g., introducing new instructional strategies). Likewise, leaders at Kelly School used a traditional management routine (the development of lesson plans focused on state standards) but connected this routine to their leadership efforts. In this case, leaders used understanding about students' mastery of course material from the skill chart to press teachers to respond proactively to students' academic needs. This explicit connection between teachers' practices and students' outcomes was used in an effort to raise teachers' individual and collective responsibility for student learning.

The distinction between management and leadership is helpful analytically, for both practitioners and researchers, but in practice they play out in tandem. The cases in this volume suggest that more work is needed to understand the relationship between management and leadership in practice.

The *Practice* of Leading and Managing

Each of the cases in this volume is anchored in the practice of leading and managing the schoolhouse. This should come as no surprise given the centrality of practice when taking a distributed perspective to frame research. The cases provide in-depth analyses of the practice of leading and managing and do so in a rather particular way. Looking across the cases, a number of common themes emerge with respect to the practice of leading and managing. In these cases, practice is not reduced to a set of behaviors or actions that can be extracted from place and time. Certainly readers can take some lessons about practice from a particular case. From Halverson's case, a reader might extract some strategies that leaders might put into practice that might contribute to building professional community in a school, or from Diamond's case, one might draw some ideas about those strategies that might raise teachers' expectations for students and develop a sense of responsibility for student learning among staff.

Readers also might extract some lessons about practice by comparing across cases. For instance, some strategies for using testing data and monitoring students' mastery of instructional material might be extracted from the cases of Kelly and Adams Schools. Leaders at Kelly School used the skill chart to connect teachers' lesson planning and instructional practices with state standards and the skills students needed to be successful on standardized tests. Likewise, the Adams Five-Week Assessment process linked standards, lesson planning, and a systematic approach to monitoring student learning. The cases surface some of these strategies and, more important, document their use in practice.

Some readers might define these behaviors or strategies as practices. We don't want to get bogged down on the semantics, but we do want to make clear that documenting these strategies or practices falls short of analyzing the practice of leading and managing. The cases show this in a number of ways. These cases underscore that studying the practice of leading and managing involves more than extracting behaviors or strategies from an analysis of practice in one situation for whole-cloth transfer to another situation. As the cases illustrate, practice is embedded in time. Although this temporal aspect of practice often is taken for granted, it is essential when analyzing practice (Bourdieu, 1990). Practice unfolds in time. Something happens, people act, but only in relation to others, and it is in these interactions that practice takes form. The best-laid plans, grand designs, or well-learned strategies often turn out very different *in practice*. In Chapter 6, Sherer captures how the Five-Week Assessment routine, as designed and intended by school leaders, turned out rather different as it unfolded over time in day-to-day practice at Adams School. Some readers might argue that this was a result of weak implementation of the organizational routine—different components of the routine were ignored, the routine was understaffed, and so on. But such an analysis misses the temporal and positional dimension of practice. Because practice cannot be fully understood outside of its relation to time and space, it is necessary to understand how it is embedded in context.

Moreover, as practice unfolds in the present, it is never really free of the past. Take the Costen case (Chapter 5) by way of example. Hallett's account documents Mrs. Kox's attempts to implement new organizational routines, for instance, actively monitoring classroom instruction, in an effort to fundamentally change leadership and management practice at Costen. These were routines that Mrs. Kox gleaned from her prior experience and her principal preparation program. She worked at putting them into practice, but she did not act in a vacuum; she acted in relation to others, and it was in these interactions that the practice of leading and managing unfolded at Costen. Especially striking in the Costen case is how these interactions—including the reactions of some staff to Mrs. Kox's actions—were fundamentally influenced by the past. At Costen, teachers were accustomed to having substantial autonomy in their classrooms. The leaders who preceded Mrs. Kox saw their role as buffering teachers from external influences and were comfortable allowing teachers to determine their own instructional practices. However, given the district's push toward accountability and Mrs. Kox's sense that she needed to be a more hands-on instructional leader, conflict arose. While practice unfolds in the present, those involved bring a logic that frames their interactions. This is what Bourdieu (1990) terms the logic of practice—a logic that "is able to organize all thoughts, perceptions, and actions by means of a few generative principles" (p. 86).

People's logic emerges from a life of negotiating social situations and is realized in ongoing interactions through a "regulated improvisation" (Bourdieu, 1977). At Costen, many teachers, especially veteran teachers, had developed a logic over years working with prior administrations. They had grown accustomed to being left to their own devices, closing their doors and teaching, and a school leadership and management practice that protected them from external interference. They brought this logic to their interactions with Mrs. Kox. Again time is key here, as improvisation is as much about responding to what came before—the past—as it is about dealing with the immediate moment—the present. A list of the behaviors that Mrs. Kox engaged in or the routines she implemented would have failed to capture the nature of leading and managing practice.

Taken together, these cases show that simply extracting behaviors or strategies from their place and time is insufficient in understanding leadership and management practice. Such endeavors have their place. For example, these cases offer a set of organizational routines, even behaviors or strategies, that schools might use to address various organizational functions such as building a professional community, raising teachers' expectations for students, and teacher development. Some readers may take these routines, strategies, and behaviors and work on putting them into practice in other sites. But our analyses show how these routines and strategies are embedded in particular places and times, and our work unearths the interdependencies that are part and parcel of practice as it unfolds in time. Hence, a critical lesson from these cases, more critical than the components of any one routine, is appreciation for interdependencies of practice that are critical when any of these routines play out in particular places and times.

Another issue that these cases bring to the surface is that investigating practice entails working on multiple planes of analysis simultaneously. Some of these cases move back and forth from the here-and-now, minute-by-minute interactions of a particular organizational routine to situating this routine in a system of practice as part of a system of organizational routines. Other cases move from analyzing practice in a particular place and time to connecting it to the past by tracing its origins and evolution over time.

Rethinking Followers

A distributed perspective casts followers as one of three core constituting elements of the practice of leading and managing. As one might expect, followers figure prominently in many of these cases, which generate insights into how followers define leadership practice and the connection between leadership and instructional practice. In Chapter 4, for example, Ms. Grant (a first-year teacher) plays the conventional role of a follower. She heeds the advice of school administrators and her mentor teacher and implements their suggestions with her students. Understanding how followers make sense of leaders' efforts and how leadership practice is translated into classroom practices is an important lens through which to view these relationships.

In Chapter 5, we are presented with an altogether different image of followers. Hallett shows how teachers at Costen with no formally designated leadership positions fundamentally shape the leadership practice at the school by virtue of becoming informal leaders. In this case, we see followers move in and out of leader roles depending on the situation. In this conflict-ridden context, they emerge as leaders of organizational rebellion rather than as compliant implementers of school leaders' instructional agendas. Likewise, in Chapter 4, we saw how some teachers worked against school leaders' desire to raise expectations for students and build a strong sense of responsibility for student learning among teachers. As the principal at Kelly school observed, some teachers engaged in informal exchanges (e.g., lunchroom conversations) that blamed students and their families for low student achievement and downplayed teachers' responsibility for student learning.

In Chapters 6 and 7, Sherer and Burch show how followers, by virtue of how they interact with leaders in organizational routines, contribute to defining leadership practice. But because followers interacted differently with one another and with leaders in mathematics compared with language arts, the practice of leading and managing looks different depending on the school subject. Followers are central to defining the practice of leading and managing, although in different ways in language arts than in mathematics. In language arts, followers more actively participate in shaping organizational routines than in mathematics. They interject ideas, challenge others' perspectives, and contribute to a lively and robust discourse about language arts instruction. In mathematics, they are more likely to defer to others (either internal or external to the organization) who they feel have specific expertise. These patterns fundamentally shape the form of leadership and management practice related to mathematics compared with leadership and management practice related to language arts.

Situation and Leadership Practice

As discussed above in the context of followers, from a distributed perspective, aspects of the situation are critical when it comes to understanding the practice of leading and managing. Each of the cases treats the situation as a defining or constituting element of practice. As a collection, the cases underscore the importance of treating aspects of the situation or context not merely as aids to, or accessories for, practice but as core constituting elements of that practice. Each case generates rather different insights into how the situation contributes to defining the practice of leading and managing the school, in part by focusing on different aspects of the situation. Further, the cases help flesh out how it is that a tool or routine or some other aspect of the situation can contribute to defining practice.

Chapters 6 and 7 focus on the school subject as one aspect of the situation and illuminate how what is being led and managed—teaching and learning in particular curricular domains—contributes to defining the practice of leading and managing. In doing so, Sherer and Burch make a convincing case for treating teaching and learning not purely as outcome variables but also as potentially powerful explanatory variables in studies of school leadership and management. School subjects—mathematics, language arts, and so on—provide a set of resources and norms that contribute to shaping the day-to-day practice of leading and managing schools. These resources and norms differ both qualitatively and quantitatively depending on the school subject. As discussed above, the human resources embedded in the organization differ by subject matter. In both cases, more leaders emerged to support teachers' work in language arts instruction than in mathematics. Leaders were more likely to use homegrown resources in language arts and externally generated resources in mathematics.

Focusing on leading and managing within writing instruction, the Hillside case illuminates how two other aspects of the situation—organizational routines and tools—contribute to defining the practice of leading and managing. The writing folder review routine, together with the tools of students writing samples, teachers' grading, and comments on students work, served as go-betweens, or mediators, in the principal's interactions with teachers and students about writing instruction. As Coldren highlights in the Hillside case, leadership and management tools contribute to defining practice in two ways. First, tools frame and focus interactions among teachers and school leaders in particular ways. With respect to the writing folder review routines, the tools (students' writing samples and teachers' commentary on these samples) focused the interaction on what children actually could write and teachers' evaluation of this writing. Other tools, such as teachers' lesson plans used in isolation, would have focused the interactions in a different way. Second, the writing folder review routine allowed the school principal at Hillside to interact simultaneously with both students and their teachers about writing instruction and its improvement. Many routines for managing and leading instruction focus chiefly on the teacher and neglect students. By framing and focusing the interactions among leaders and followers in particular ways, routines and tools give form to leadership and management practice.

These tools and routines at Hillside were shaped in part by another aspect of the situation—school size. With well over 1,000 students at Hillside, Mrs. Nelson established routines that allowed her to obtain substantive information about what was going on in her teachers' classrooms without requiring extensive time to observe them frequently. In this way, school size represents a constituting element of school leadership and management.

Another aspect of the situation is the racial and social class composition of the schools' students. In the schools we studied, most students are low income and of color. Because low-income, Black, and Latino/a students often are assumed to be less academically capable than White students, teachers sometimes expect less of them academically and of themselves as teachers (Diamond, Randolph, & Spillane, 2004). Leadership in such schools often means establishing routines that combat these low expectations. In Chapter 4, Diamond shows how leaders use formal organizational routines to raise both teachers' expectations of students and their own sense of responsibility for student learning. Such routines are less necessary in schools with different student compositions. In this way, the student composition of schools is a constituting element of leading and managing schools.

In Chapter 5, Hallett takes up different aspects of the situation at Costen: the school's recent history and the district policy environment. The district's high-stakes accountability policy, the pressure for rapid change brought on by the Local School Council, and the principal's instructional improvement philosophy combined to create a level of urgency for school change and principal activism that conflicted with the history of teacher autonomy with regard to classroom work.

At the same time, the cases show how aspects of the situation get created and recreated in the practice of leading and managing. As the Hillside case makes clear, the writing folder review routine and its accompanying tools were created through leadership practice. In Chapter 3, Halverson discussed how the establishment of organizational routines (particularly Breakfast Club) created conditions that enhanced professional community among teachers. In the Kelly case presented in Chapter 4, Diamond shows how leadership practice can help define the situation by shaping school discourse regarding students' ability and teachers' responsibility for student learning.

The situation or context, as scholars refer to it, is a loose term difficult to pin down and irritatingly difficult to unravel in terms of its influence on practice. Each of the cases in this volume pinpoints different aspects of the situation as these become instantiated in practice and explores how these aspects structure that practice. In this way, the cases bring alive how aspects of the situation—routines, tools, school subjects—contribute to defining the daily practice of leading and managing by framing and focusing the interactions among leaders.

Attending to the Designed and Lived Organization in Tandem

Although formal leadership and management arrangements have consumed much of the literature in education, scholars of leadership and management also have recognized the importance of informal leadership. Further, most accounts tend to focus on one or the other—either the formal or the informal organization. A distributed perspective on leadership and management as illustrated in these cases offers a lens for looking at the designed and lived organization in tandem. Both are critical to understanding the work of leading and managing the schoolhouse. Diamond's account in Chapter 4, for example, shows how formal routines are used to raise teachers' expectations for students and their sense of responsibility for student learning. Similarly, Sherer's case illustrates that whereas the organizational routines as designed can look relatively similar for language arts and mathematics, things turn out rather different in practice—in the organization as lived.

A distributed perspective, however, does more than argue for attention to both the designed and lived organization. From a distributed perspective, the designed and lived organization must be understood in tandem—together, in interaction! You can't understand the one without the other. Hallett's account of Mrs. Kox's efforts to lead change at Costen through the creation of new organizational routines (the designed organization) would be seriously lacking if it had not attended to the lived organization at Costen and the efforts of some veteran teachers with no formal leadership designations.

Moreover, the distributed perspective offers a way of conceptualizing or framing relations between the organization as designed and the organization as lived. Aspects of the designed organization—formal organizational routines, formal positions—as instantiated in daily work structure the practice of leading and managing. At the same time, these structures are a product of practice, sometimes school-level practice, other times practice beyond the schoolhouse. The Breakfast Club routine at Adams School, for example, was a product of practice at Adams. In turn, this organizational routine, once institutionalized, structured the practice of leading and managing at the school.

Leading and Managing—To What End?

Some readers may wonder about the wisdom of investing time and effort to build a richer understanding of the practice of leading and managing. Pressing for more practical lessons, they may wonder what these cases that take a distributed perspective have to do with school improvement. Each of these cases is firmly tied to the work of leadership and management as it relates to different aspects of school improvement, from building professional community among staff to monitoring instruction and working on teacher development.

Chapters 2, 4, and 5 highlight organizational routines designed to monitor instruction and promote teacher development. Current reform efforts seek fundamental changes in teachers' instructional practices in terms of both the content they teach and the pedagogic practices they use. Understanding the link between leadership and instruction as it plays out daily in schools is a critical component of understanding this change process. In Chapter 2, Coldren shows how organizational routines she calls boundary practices allowed the principal, Barbara Nelson, to gain insight into instructional practice at Hillside and how that helped her influence teachers' practices. With the use of boundary objects like the writing folders and lesson plans, leaders at Hillside were able to bridge the traditional divide between administration and the classroom. The skill chart played a similar role in Kelly School (Chapter 4). It provided insight into classroom instructional practice and student learning and became a tool used by school leaders to influence teachers' beliefs and practices. In Chapter 5, Hallett highlights the tenuous nature of administrators' connections to the classroom by showing how Costen's teachers initially rebuffed the principal's efforts to establish new routines.

In Chapter 3, Halverson contributes to our understanding of how professional community is developed by detailing the role that organizational routines play in building professional community. Strong professional community is thought to be a critical component of school improvement. Absent a fine-grained analysis of how improvement is cultivated in schools, however, we cannot move from knowing that we need it to bringing it about. Halverson's work documents the leadership practice that created the conditions for professional community to develop among teachers.

In Chapter 4, Diamond analyzes the practice of leading and managing improvement efforts designed to transform teachers' beliefs about and expectations for students (a critical component in addressing inequality). Again, in this chapter, the analysis moves beyond documenting low expectations or arguing for raising them to actually unpacking how school leaders at Kelly addressed this issue in the day-to-day work at the school. Diamond highlights a set of interconnected routines that, taken together, contribute to practice and discourse that reinforce high expectations for students and a strong commitment on the part of teachers to engage in instructional practices that meet all students' needs.

Both the Adams and Baxter cases document how the work of leading and managing school improvement is not generic but school subject specific. Sherer and Burch show through their respective cases that the constellation of leaders, the nature of the interactions in performing organizational routines, and the ways in which tools are used differ for instruction in mathematics as compared with language arts. These cases, chronicled in Chapters 6 and 7, provide compelling evidence that the school subject matter is a critical consideration in our efforts to understand the practice of leading and managing, even in elementary schools. These cases suggest that in analyzing and working to improve school leadership and management, it is important to think carefully about school subjects and how they might structure the work differently.

A critical issue in any discussion of school leadership and management considers whether and how it connects with the core work of schooling—that is, teaching and learning. This is in part a question of impact, but it involves more than impact because it also concerns uncovering the theory of action. Specifically, how are particular organizational routines meant to enable improvement in teaching and learning?

The cases help uncover possible pathways from the practice of leading and managing to instructional practice, making explicit connections between instructional practice and school leadership and management. Some organizational routines, for example, chiefly target the teacher and the curricular materials, such as Literacy Committee meetings at Adams and Baxter Schools or professional development meetings at Kelly. Other routines focus chiefly on students, such as the Real Men Read routine at Adams (see Appendix 3.1), specifically designed to encourage African American male students to engage in more reading by providing them with African American male role models. The cultural relevance routines at Kelly School, which included the Black national anthem, a Black history fact, and an affirming school pledge, were designed to build a positive environment for African American students and to reinforce students' beliefs in their capacity for high achievement. These routines were designed by school leaders to combat the broader local and societal discourse that often raises questions about African Americans' intellectual capacity (Diamond, forthcoming; Perry, Steele, & Hilliard, 2003).

Other routines target both students and teachers simultaneously. For example, the writing folder review routine at Hillside connects with teachers and students simultaneously about writing instruction. As an organizational routine, it targets both teachers and students on the same topic. Looking across these chapters, we can begin to identify various ways in which leadership management practice might connect with instructional practice, through students, materials, teachers, or some combination of these factors.

MOVING FORWARD: CHALLENGES WHEN TAKING A DISTRIBUTED PERSPECTIVE IN RESEARCH AND DEVELOPMENT

Research on leadership and management from a distributed perspective is still very much preadolescent. Much work remains to be done. We see at least two broad lines of research work: (1) theory building and the generation of tenable hypotheses and (2) hypotheses testing. Both will involve epistemological and methodological challenges. An additional challenge that we believe researchers need to take on is the challenge of making their conceptual and methodological tools available to and useful for those working in the practice of leading and managing. More specifically, researchers in applied fields such as education need to consider whether and how their conceptual and methodological tools can be designed in such ways that they can be used by school leaders and those who work on leadership and management development. We take up these three issues here.

Theory Building

Relatively few scholars have taken up the challenge of theory building around *the practice aspect* of a distributed perspective. Most of the work continues to focus on the leader plus aspect. Many important questions remain to be teased out, and there is a need for more studies to see whether patterns identified hold across schools and across particular populations of schools.

For example, do the subject-matter differences in leadership practice in elementary schools identified in Chapters 6 and 7 hold in other elementary schools? Similarly, much of the work on distributed leadership has focused on primary or elementary schools. Hence a critical question concerns how leadership is distributed in secondary schools. Investigating leadership practice from a distributed perspective at the secondary-school level poses a distinctly different challenge. At the secondary level, the subject-specific departmental structure is critical, and departmental chairs or heads are unique. Therefore, the distinctive cultures of subject-area departments will be especially important in studying leadership and management from a distributed perspective at the secondary level. Work of this sort is essential in order to generate tenable hypotheses, essential for theory-testing work.

Of course, theory-building work can have very practical implications. Empirical studies within the distributed framework outlined in this book can give insights on the improvement of school leadership and management. A distributed perspective offers a new meta-lens for investigating leadership and management practice, providing a set of analytical tools for generating rich cases of that practice. By providing a frame that helps researchers build cases for practitioners to interpret and think about in their ongoing leadership and management practice, the distributed perspective offers a tool to help researchers and practitioners work on improving practice together. For example, thinking about tools as critical elements of practice might press school leaders to consider the tools they use and how these tools both enable and constrain their practice.

Theory Testing and Questions of Effectiveness

Some bemoan the weak empirical knowledge base on distributed leadership. But this is to be expected considering that the ideas are relatively new. In the current climate, many education researchers have rushed headlong into questions of effectiveness, naïvely interpreting the recent press in education circles for research designs that allow for strong causal inferences. Education certainly could benefit from more randomized trials or quasi-experimental designs that allow for more robust causal inferences. But, as any savvy researcher would point out, including the strongest advocates for more randomized trials in education research, it is troublesome to design research to gauge the effectiveness of something that is fuzzy. Indeed, it is not only troublesome; it is foolhardy.

Hence, more theory-building and hypothesis-generating work is imperative before measuring the effects on teaching and student learning. At this stage in the game, expecting to have an empirically sound knowledge base on the effectiveness of distributed leadership is little more than wishful thinking. Further, as we argued in Chapter 1, a distributed take on leadership and management is not a prescription for effective leadership in and of itself; what is likely to be most salient in trying to tease out the effects of distributed leadership is not *that* leadership is distributed, but *how* leadership is distributed. The sort of theory-building and hypothesis-generating work currently underway is an important precursor to hypothesis-testing research and any serious attempts at tackling questions of effectiveness.

In moving forward, a number of methodological and epistemological challenges will have to be met if the field wishes to develop a solid empirical knowledge base about school leadership and management from a distributed perspective. One of these challenges concerns the identification of leadership and management in schools. Currently, investigators and practitioners rely on labor-intensive and costly ethnographic and structured observation methods to identify leadership and management practice. While these methods generate rich insights into leadership and management practice, they typically are limited by small sample sizes that make it difficult to generalize to a population of schools. Hence, these approaches on their own are limited for evaluation research and for generating robust empirical evidence about relations between leadership and management development, leadership and management practice, and classroom practice. Developing valid and reliable ways to identify leadership and management practice is difficult because this practice potentially spans the entire school building, involving the work of not only formally designated leaders but also individuals with no such designations. Further, leadership and management practice ordinarily is not confined to structured and patterned time slots; it happens before and after school, on weekends, and during school hours both in formally designated routines such as grade-level meetings and during informal interactions over lunch or in exchanges snatched between classes. Although challenging, the task of developing more robust means of identifying leadership and management practice is not insurmountable.

Identifying leadership—and management practice—is one thing. Developing instruments for documenting it systematically across large samples of schools is another matter. To date, scholars and practitioners have relied on either costly ethnographic and structured observational methods or surveys. Both suffer from distinctly different problems. The first approach typically is too expensive for more than a handful of schools. The second approach often employs instruments that are too crude to capture the nuances of leadership practice, especially the differences between reported practice and actual practice. A key challenge for scholars of leadership and management practice will involve developing instruments that allow us to capture leadership and management practice across large samples of schools.

Making Methodological and Analytical Tools Practitioner Friendly

A different sort of challenge for those working in applied fields such as education concerns the usability of our conceptual and methodological tools in practice (Spillane, 2006). Standard operating procedure generates robust empirical evidence and then leaves others to translate it for practitioners. Somehow research findings will find their way to practitioners and thereby inform practice. The available evidence suggests that this model does not work very well. Empirical findings often do not reach practitioners or, if they do find their way into practice, they have little impact on improving that practice. We believe that the dissemination model has fundamental flaws. Conceptual and empirical findings are, more often than not, lost in translation. Some of this may be inevitable, but we believe that the research community can do more.

To begin with, concepts and ideas—such as the distributed perspective—can be represented in ways that are more or less practitioner friendly. Theory is a dirty word for many practitioners, and for good reason. Those who build theory do not engage the difficult work of relating their theory in a user-friendly way to the world of practitioners, especially relating it to their daily practice.

Further, methodological tools can be tailored so that practitioners can evaluate and appreciate the usefulness to their work and potentially use the tools in their practice. For example, over the past few years, we have used data from a leadership identification instrument—social network survey—as a way of getting school leaders to think through where leadership is in their organization. This work involves more than simply reporting the findings from our research; it involves developing situations where practitioners can engage with these data and then make connections to their own schools. In addition, we currently are working on redesigning these instruments and logs so that practitioners can use them to study their own schools.

To date, a distributed perspective has offered new insights into the work of leading and managing the schoolhouse. Of course, there is much work to be done, especially in the empirical arena. We have had plenty of armchair theorizing about distributed leadership, indeed leadership and management writ large. Theory has its place and is indeed a good friend and essential for strong empirical work. But more empirical work, both theory generating and hypothesis testing, is critical. Indeed, we suspect that future theorizing about a distributed perspective on school leadership and management will be much more fruitful if grounded in empirical work.

Notes

Chapter 2

1. All names have been changed.
2. Although I recognize the political nature of principals' work, for this chapter I focus primarily on their instructional and managerial roles.
3. While some educators agree that an emphasis on standardized tests can lead to positive school improvements, others caution that such an emphasis on testing is misguided and inevitably leads to "teaching to the test." My purpose is not to condone or condemn standardized testing but rather to illustrate how assessments as a tool helped shape leadership practice at Hillside.
4. The annual ISAT was scheduled to be administered in the coming weeks.

Chapter 4

Research on this chapter was supported by the National Academy of Education and the National Academy of Education/Spencer Foundation Postdoctoral Fellowship Program. Previous versions of the paper on which this chapter is based were presented at the 2004 American Educational Research Association Conference. All opinions and conclusions expressed in this paper are those of the author and do not necessarily reflect the views of any funding agency or institution.

1. All names of people and institutions used in this chapter are pseudonyms.

Chapter 5

1. LSCs were created in 1985 as part of reforms premised on school-based governance. When these reforms did not increase test scores, the Mayor of Chicago centralized control, appointing a "Chief Executive Officer" of city schools and giving birth to accountability. However, LSCs remained part of the system, operating under the umbrella of accountability. The task of the LSC is to review school policies, approve a budget and an academic enhancement plan that fits city standards

and goals, and hire and evaluate the principal. At Costen School the LSC was viewed as, and viewed itself as, an agent of accountability that was external to the school.

2. The only exception was student records.

3. Indeed, my knowledge of this prior order developed over the course of a year of observations and interviews with teachers.

4. And in the past Korean, Assyrian, Guajarati, and Arabic.

5. Percent of students coming in and out of the school during the school year.

6. I have selected these as examples because they are relatively straightforward and can be briefly described within space limitations. However, there were a number of other changes that I document in a larger account of the school (Hallett, 2003).

7. It is a notable irony that the teachers say they need flexibility, but then they are not flexible enough to adapt to new policies. The issue is not really flexibility, but rather autonomy and control (Ingersoll, 2003).

8. (1) Fewer than 37% of students with limited English proficiency met or exceeded state reading standards, (2) fewer than 37% of students with limited English proficiency met or exceeded state math standards, (3) fewer than 37% of disabled students met or exceeded state reading standards, (4) fewer than 95% of Asian students were tested in reading, (5) fewer than 95% of Asian students were tested in math, (6) fewer than 95% of low-income students were tested in reading, and (7) fewer than 95% of low-income students were tested in math.

Chapter 7

1. Initially, I sought to observe and better understand the range of leadership activities and structures at Baxter by observing meetings of the Local School Council, the leadership group, cycle meetings, as well as conferences between school administrators. As differences by subject area around instructional reforms moved to the foreground, I began observations of the 5th- to 8th-grade, subject-specific workgroups and observed other leadership structures and sampled meetings where subject-matter issues would be addressed. I used a postobservation interview to elicit school participants' perspectives on the meetings observed.

References

Argyris, C. (1990). *Overcoming organizational defenses: Facilitating organizational learning*. Boston: Allyn & Bacon.

Ball, S. J. (1981). *Beachside comprehensive*. Cambridge: Cambridge University Press.

Ball, S. J. (1987). *The micro-politics of the school: Towards a theory of school organization*. London: Methuen.

Ball, S. J., & Lacey, C. (1995). Revisiting subject disciplines as the opportunity for group action: A measured critique of subject subcultures. In L. S. Siskin & J. W. Little (Eds.), *The subjects in question* (pp. 95–122). New York: Teachers College Press.

Bidwell, C. E. (1965). The school as a formal organization. In J. March (Ed.), *Handbook of organizations* (pp. 972–1022). Chicago: Rand McNally.

Bossert, S. T., Dwyer, D., Rowan, B., & Lee, G. V. (1982). The instructional management role of the principal. *Educational Administration Quarterly, 18*(3), 34–63.

Bourdieu, P. (1977). *Outline of a theory of practice*. Cambridge, UK: Cambridge University Press.

Bourdieu, P. (1981). The specificity of the scientific field. In C. Lemert (Ed.), *French sociology: Rupture and renewal since 1968* (pp. 6–96). New York: Columbia University Press.

Bourdieu, P. (1990). *The logic of practice*. Stanford: Stanford University Press.

Bryk, A. S., & Driscoll, M. E. (1985). *An empirical investigation of the school as community*. Chicago: University of Chicago, School of Education.

Bryk, A. S., Bebring, P. B., Kerbow, D., Rollow, S., & Easton, J. Q. (1996). Catalyzing basic organizational change at the building level. In *Charting Chicago-school reform* (pp. 93–129). Chicago: Westview Press.

Bryk, A. S., & Schneider, B. (2002). *Trust in schools: A core resource for improvement*. New York: Russell Sage.

Burch, P., & Spillane, J. P. (2003). Elementary school leadership strategies and subject matter: Reforming mathematics and literacy instruction. *The Elementary School Journal, 103*(5), 519–535.

Burch, P., & Spillane, J. P. (2005). How subjects matter in district office practice: Instructionally relevant policy in urban school district redesign. *Journal of Educational Change, 6*(1), 51–76.

Burns, J. M. (1978). *Leadership.* New York: Harper & Row.

Cobb, P., & McClain, K. (2005, April). *The collective mediation of a high stakes accountability program: Communities and networks of practice.* Paper presented at the annual meeting of the American Educational Research Association, Montreal.

Cobb, P. S., McClain, K., & Gravemeijer, K. (2001). Participating in classroom mathematical practices. *Journal of the Learning Sciences, 10,* 113–164.

Coburn, C. (2005, August). *Framing social problems at the school site: Using frame analysis to uncover the micro-processes of policy implementation.* Paper presented at the Sociology of Education session at the annual meeting of the American Sociological Association, Philadelphia.

Cohen, D. K., & Ball, D. L. (1998). *Instruction, capacity, and improvement* (CPRE Research Report Series, RR-42). Philadelphia: University of Pennsylvania, CPRE.

Coleman, J. S. (1988). Social capital in the creation of human capital. *American Journal of Sociology, 94,* 95–120.

Consortium on Chicago School Research. (1998). *Improving Chicago's schools.* Chicago: Author.

Correa, M., Easton, J., Johnson, O., Ponisciak, S., & Rosenkranz, T. (2004). *Selected indicators from the U.S. census and Chicago public schools records related to the lives and schooling of children.* Chicago: Consortium on Chicago School Research.

Cuban, L. (1988). *The managerial imperative and the practice of leadership in schools.* Albany: State University of New York Press.

Cunningham, P. M., Hall, D. P., & Defee, M. (1998). Nonability grouped, multilevel instruction: Eight years later. *Reading Teacher, 51,* 652–664.

Diamond, J. B. (forthcoming). Cultivating a school-based discourse that emphasizes teachers' responsibility for student learning. In M. Pollock (Ed.), *Everyday antiracism: Concrete ways to successfully navigate the relevance of race in school.* New York: New Press.

Diamond, J. B., Randolph, A., & Spillane, J. P. (2004). Teachers' expectations and sense of responsibility for student learning: The implications of school race, class, and organizational habitus. *Anthropology and Education Quarterly, 35*(1), 75–98.

Dwyer, D. C., Lee, G., Rowan, B., & Bossert, S. (1983). *Five principals in action: Perspectives on instructional management.* San Francisco: Far West Laboratory for Educational Research.

Easton, J. Q., Correa, M., Luppescu, S., Park, H.-S., Ponisciak, S., & Rosenkranz, T. (2003). *How do they compare? ITBS and ISAT reading and mathematics in the Chicago public schools, 1999–2002* (Research Data Brief). Chicago: Consortium on Chicago School Research.

Eccles, R. G., & Nohria, N. (1992). *Beyond the hype: Rediscovering the essence of management.* Boston: Harvard Business School Press.

Ehrlich, S. B. (1998). Leader-centric and follower-centric research at multiple levels of analysis: Toward a balanced perspective. *Monographs in Organizational Behavior and Industrial Relations, 24,* 303–309.

Feldman, M. S. (2000). Organizational routines as a source of continuous change. *Organization Science, 11*(6), 611–629.

Feldman, M. S., & Pentland, B. T. (2003). Reconceptualizing organizational routines as a source of flexibility and change. *Administrative Science Quarterly, 48*(1), 94–118.

Ferguson, R. (1998). Teacher perceptions and expectations and the black–white test score gap. In C. Jencks & M. Philips (Eds.), *The Black–White test score gap* (pp. 273–317). Washington, DC: Brookings Institution Press.

Firestone, W. A. (1996). Leadership roles of functions? In K. Leithwood, J. Chapman, D. Corson, P. Hallinger, & A. Hart (Eds.), *International handbook of educational leadership and administration* (Vol. 2, pp. 395–418). Boston: Kluwer Academic.

Firestone, W. A., & Martinez, C. (2007). Districts, teacher leaders, and distributed leadership: Changing instructional practice. *Leadership and Policy in Schools, 6,* 3–35.

Fowler, F. C. (1999). Curiouser and curiouser: New concepts in the rapidly changing landscape of educational administration. *Educational Administration Quarterly, 35*(4), 594–613.

Frost, D. (2005). Resisting the juggernaut: Building capacity through teacher leadership in spite of it all. *Leading and Managing, 10*(2), 83.

Galbraith, J. R. (1973). *Designing complex organizations.* Reading, MA: Addison-Wesley.

Gladwell, M. (2000). *The tipping point: How little things can make a big difference.* Boston: Little Brown.

Goldring, E., & Cohen-Vogel, L. (1999, April). *Supporting environments for instructional reform: The principal's role in a new century.* Paper presented at the annual meeting of the American Educational Research Association, Montreal.

Gouldner, A. (1954). *Patterns of industrial bureaucracy.* Glencoe, IL: Free Press.

Gronn, P. (2002). Distributed leadership as a unit of analysis. *Leadership Quarterly, 13,* 423–451.

Gronn, P. (2003). *The new work of educational leaders: Changing leadership practice in an era of school reform.* London: Paul Chapman Publishing.

Grossman, P., Wineburg, S., & Woolworth, S. (2000). *What makes teacher community different from a gathering of teachers?* Seattle: Center for the Study of Teaching and Policy.

Hallett, T. (2003). *Symbolic power and the social organization of turmoil: Order, disruption, and conflict in an urban elementary school.* Unpublished doctoral dissertation, Northwestern University, Evanston, IL.

Hallinger, P., & Heck, R. H. (1996a). The principal's role in school effectiveness: An assessment of methodological progress, 1980–1995. In K. Leitherwood, J. Chapman, D. Corson, P. Hallinger, & A. Hart (Eds.), *International handbook of educational leadership and administration* (pp. 723–783). Boston: Kluwer Academic.

Hallinger, P., & Heck, R. H. (1996b). Reassessing the principal's role in school effectiveness: A review of the empirical research. *Educational Administration Quarterly, 32*(1), 5–44.

Hallinger, P., & Heck, R. H. (1998). Exploring the principal's contribution to school effectiveness. *School Effectiveness and School Improvement, 9,* 157–191.

Hallinger, P., & Murphy, J. (1987a). Instructional leadership in the school context. In W. Greenfield (Ed.), *Instructional leadership: Concepts, issues, and controversies* (pp. 179–203). Boston: Allyn & Bacon.

Hallinger, P., & Murphy, J. (1987b). The social context of effective schools. *American Journal of Education, 94*(5), 328–355.

Halverson, R. (2002). *Representing phronesis: Supporting instructional leadership practice in schools.* Unpublished doctoral dissertation, Northwestern University, Evanston, IL.

Halverson, R. (2004). Accessing, documenting and communicating practical wisdom: The phronesis of school leadership practice. *American Journal of Education, 111*(1), 90–121.

Hargreaves, A. (1994). *Changing teachers, changing times.* Toronto: University of Toronto Press.

Harris, A. (2005). Distributed leadership. In B. Davies (Ed.), *The essentials of school leadership* (pp. 133–190). London: Paul Chapman Press.

Heck, R. H., & Hallinger, P. (1999). Next generation methods for the study of leadership and school improvement. In J. Murphy & K. Louis (Eds.), *Handbook of educational administration* (pp. 141–162). New York: Longman.

Heifetz, R. A. (1994). *Leadership without easy answers.* Cambridge, MA: Bellknap Press.

Heimer, C. A. (1999). Competing institutions: Law, medicine, and family in neonatal intensive care. *Law and Society Review, 33,* 17–66.

Hersey, P., & Blanchard, K. H. (1977). *Management of organizational behavior: Utilizing human resources.* Englewood Cliffs, NJ: Prentice Hall.

Huberman, M. (1995). Networks that alter teaching: Conceptualizations, exchanges and experiments. *Teachers and Teaching: Theory and Practice, 1*(2), 193–211.

Hutchins, E. (1995). *Cognition in the wild.* Cambridge, MA: MIT Press.

Ingersoll, R. M. (2003). *Who controls teachers' work? Power and accountability in America's schools.* Cambridge, MA: Harvard University Press.

Johnson, S. M. (1990). The primacy and potential of high school departments. In M. W. McLaughlin, J. E. Talbert, & N. Bascia (Eds.), *The contexts of teaching in secondary schools: Teachers' realities* (pp. 167–184). New York: Teachers College Press.

Knapp, M., Grossman, P., & Stodolsky, S. (2005, April). *Making subject matter part of the equation: The intersection of policy and content.* Paper presented at the annual meeting of the American Educational Research Association, Montreal.

Krug, S. E. (1992). Instructional leadership: A constructivist perspective. *Educational Administration Quarterly, 28*(3), 430–443.

Ladson-Billings, G. (1994). *The dreamkeepers: Successful teachers of African American students.* San Francisco: Jossey-Bass.

Latour, B. (1987). *Science in action: How to follow engineers and scientists through society.* Cambridge, MA: Harvard University Press.

Lee, V. E., & Loeb, S. (2000). School size in Chicago elementary schools: Effects on teachers' attitudes and student achievement. *American Educational Research Journal, 37,* 3–32.

Lee, V. E., & Smith, J. B. (1996). Collective responsibility for learning and its effects on gains in achievement for early secondary school students. *American Journal of Education, 104*(2), 103–147.

Lee, V. E., & Smith, J. B. (2001). *High school restructuring and student achievement.* New York: Teachers College Press.

Leinhardt, G., & Smith, D. A. (1985). Expertise in mathematics instruction: Subject matter knowledge. *Journal of Educational Psychology, 77*(3), 247–271.

Leithwood, K., Mascall, B., Strauss, T., Sacks, R., Memon, N., & Yashkina, A. (2007). Distributing leadership to make schools smarter: Taking the ego out of the system. *Leadership and Policy in Schools, 6,* 37–67.

Leont'ev, A. N. (1981). *Problems of the development of the mind.* Moscow: Progress Publishers.

Liberman, A., Falk, B., & Alexander, L. (1994). *A culture in the making: Leadership in learner-centered schools.* New York: National Center for Restructuring Education, Schools, and Teaching, Teachers College.

Little, J. W. (1982). Norms of collegiality and experimentation. *American Educational Research Journal, 19*(3), 325–340.

Little, J. W. (1995a). Contested ground: The basis of teacher leadership in two restructuring high schools. *The Elementary School Journal, 96*(1), 47–63.

Little, J. W. (1995b). Subject affiliation in high schools that restructure. In L. S. Siskin & J. W. Little (Eds.), *The subjects in question* (pp. 172–200). New York: Teachers College Press.

Little, J. W., & Bird, T. (1987). Instructional leadership "close to the classroom" in secondary schools. In W. Greenfield (Ed.), *Instructional leadership: Concepts, issues and controversies* (pp. 118–138). Boston: Allyn & Bacon.

Lortie, D. C. (1975). *School teacher.* Chicago: University of Chicago Press.

Louis, K. S., Kruse, S. D., & Bryk, A. S. (1995). Professionalism and community: What is it and why is it important in urban schools? In K. S. Louis & S. D. Kruse (Eds.), *Professionalism and community: Perspectives on reforming urban schools* (pp. 3–22). Thousand Oaks, CA: Sage.

Louis, K. S., Marks, H., & Kruse, S. D. (1996). Teachers' professional community in restructuring schools. *American Educational Research Journal, 33*(4), 757–798.

MacBeath, J. (2006). The talent enigma. *International Journal of Leadership in Education, 9*(3), 183–204.

MacBeath, J., & McGlynn, A. (2003). *Self evaluation: What's in it for schools?* London: Routledge.

MacBeath, J., Oduro, G., & Waterhouse, J. (2004). *Distributed leadership in schools.* Nottingham, UK: National College of School Leadership.

March, J. G. (1981). Footnotes to organizational change. *Administrative Science Quarterly, 26*(4), 563–577.

March, J. G., & Simon, H. A. (1958). *Organizations.* New York: Wiley.

McLaughlin, M., & Talbert, J. E. (1993). *Contexts that matter for teaching and learning.* San Francisco: Jossey-Bass.

Meindl, J. R. (1995). The romance of leadership as follower-centric theory: A social constructionist approach. *Leadership Quarterly, 6,* 329–341.

Meyer, J. W., & Rowan, B. (1977). Institutionalized organizations: Formal structure as myth and ceremony. *American Journal of Sociology, 83,* 340–363.

Meyer, J. W., & Rowan, B. (1978). The structure of educational organizations. In Marshall W. Meyer & Associates (Eds.), *Environments and Organizations* (pp. 78–109). San Francisco: Jossey-Bass.

Miller, B., Lord, B., & Dorney, J. (1994). *Staff development for teachers: A study of configurations and costs in four districts.* Newton, MA: Education Development Center.

Miskel, C., & Cosgrove, D. (1985). Leader succession in school settings. *Review of Educational Research, 55,* 87–105.

Morrill, C., Zald, M. N., & Rao, H. (2003). Covert political conflict in organizations: Challenges from below. *Annual Review of Sociology, 29,* 391–415.

Mouton, J. S., & Blake, R. R. (1984). *Synergogy: A new strategy for education, training, and development.* San Francisco: Jossey-Bass.

Murphy, J. (1991). *Restructuring schools: Capturing and assessing the phenomena.* New York: Teachers College Press.

Newmann, F., & Wehlage, G. G. (1995). *Successful school restructuring.* Alexandria, VA: Association for Supervision and Curriculum Development.

Paule, L. (1986). *The curriculum decision environment of high school English, mathematics, science, and social studies departments.* Unpublished doctoral dissertation, University of Oregon, Eugene.

Pea, R. D. (1993). Practices of distributed intelligence and designs for education. In G. Saloman (Ed.), *Distributed cognition: Psychological and educational considerations* (pp. 89–132). New York: Cambridge University Press.

Perrow, C. (1967). A framework for the comparative analysis of organizations. *American Sociological Review, 32*(2), 194–208.

Perry, T., Steele, C., & Hilliard, A. G. (2003). *Young, gifted, and black: Promoting high achievement among African-American students.* Boston: Beacon Press.

Pickering, A. (1992). *Science as practice and culture.* Chicago: University of Chicago Press.

Prestine, N. A., & Nelson, B. S. (2005). How can educational leaders support and promote teaching and learning? New conceptions of learning and leading in schools. In W. A. Firestone & C. Riehl (Eds.), *A new agenda for research in educational leadership* (pp. 46–60). New York: Teachers College Press.

Purkey, S. C., & Smith, M. S. (1983). Effective schools: A review. *Elementary School Journal, 83,* 427–452.

Resnick, L. (1991). Shared cognition: Thinking as social practice. In L. Resnick, J. Levine, & S. Teasley (Eds.), *Perspectives on socially shared cognition* (pp. 1–19). Washington, DC: American Psychological Association.

Roderick, M., & Nagaoka, J. (2004). Retention under Chicago's high-stakes testing program: Helpful, harmful, or harmless? *Educational Evaluation and Policy Analysis, 27*(4), 309–340.

Rosenholtz, S. J. (1989a). *Teachers' workplace: The social organization of schools.* New York: Longman.

Rosenholtz, S. J. (1989b). Workplace conditions that affect teacher quality and commitment: Implications for teacher induction programs. *Elementary School Journal, 89*(4), 421–439.

Rowan, B. (1990). Commitment and control: Alternative strategies for the organizational design of schools. *Review of Research in Education, 16,* 353–389.

Rowan, B. (2002a). Teachers' work and instructional management, Part I: Alternative views of the task of teaching. In W. K. Hoy & C. G. Miskel (Eds.), *Theory and research in educational administration* (Vol. 1, pp. 129–149). Greenwich, CT: Information Age.

Rowan, B. (2002b). Teachers' work and instructional management, Part II: Does organic management promote expert teaching? In W. K. Hoy & C. G. Miskel (Eds.), *Theory and research in educational administration* (Vol. 1, pp. 151–168). Greenwich, CT: Information Age.

Schneider, B. (1998). There IS some there there. *Monographs in Organizational Behavior and Industrial Relations, 24,* 311–319.

Scott, W. R. (1995). *Institutions and organizations.* Thousand Oaks, CA: Sage.

Siskin, L. S. (1991a). Departments as different worlds: Subject subcultures in secondary schools. *Educational Administration Quarterly, 27*(2), 134–160.

Siskin, L. S. (1991b). *School restructuring and subject subcultures.* Stanford, CA: Center for Research on the Context of Secondary Teaching.

Siskin, L. S. (1994). *Realms of knowledge: Academic departments in secondary schools.* Washington, DC: Falmer Press.

Slavin, R. E., & Madden, N. A. (2001). *One million children: Success for all.* Thousand Oaks, CA: Corwin Press.

Spillane, J. P. (2005). Primary school leadership practice: How the subject matters. *School Leadership and Management, 25*(4), 383–397.

Spillane, J. P. (2006). *Distributed leadership.* San Francisco: Jossey-Bass.

Spillane, J. P., & Burch, P. (2004). *The institutional environment and the technical core in K–12 schools: "Loose coupling" revisited.* Available at http://www.northwestern.edu/ipr/publications/papers/2003/wp-03-04.pdf

Spillane, J. P., & Burch, P. (2006). The institutional environment and instructional practice: Changing patterns of guidance and control in public schools. In H. Meir & B. Rowan (Eds.), *The new institutionalism in education.* Albany: State University of New York Press.

Spillane, J. P., Diamond, J., Burch, P., Hallett, T., Jita, L., & Zoltners, J. (2002). Managing in the middle: School leadership and the enactment of accountability. *Educational Policy, 16,* 731–762.

Spillane, J. P., Diamond, J. B., & Jita, L. (2000, April). *Leading classroom instruction: A preliminary exploration of the distribution of leadership.* Paper presented at the annual meeting of the American Educational Research Association, New Orleans.

Spillane, J. P., Diamond, J.B., & Jita, L. (2003). Leading instruction: The distribution of leadership for instruction. *Journal of Curriculum Studies, 35,* 533–543.

Spillane, J. P., Hallett, T., & Diamond, J. (2003). Forms of capital and the construction of leadership: Instructional leadership in urban elementary schools. *Sociology of Education, 76,* 1–17.

Spillane, J. P., Halverson, R., & Diamond, J. B. (2001). Investigating school leadership practice: A distributed perspective. *Educational Researcher, 30*(3), 23–27.

Spillane, J. P., Halverson, R., & Diamond, J. (2004). Towards a theory of school leadership practice: Implications of a distributed perspective. *Journal of Curriculum Studies, 36,* 3–34.

Star, S. L. (1989). The structure of ill-structured solutions: Boundary objects and heterogeneous distributed problem solving. In L. Gasser & M. N. Huhns (Eds.), *Distributed artificial intelligence* (Vol. 2, pp. 37–54). London: Pitman.

Star, S. L., & Griesemer, J. R. (1989). Institutional ecology, "translations," and boundary objects: Amateurs and professionals in Berkeley's Museum of Vertebrate Zoology, 1907–39. *Social Studies of Science, 19,* 387–420.

Stein, M. K., & D'Amico, L. (1999). *Leading school and district-wide reform: Multiple subjects matter* (Report on content driven reform). Pittsburgh, PA: University of Pittsburgh.

Stein, M. K., & D'Amico, L. (2002). Inquiry at the crossroads of policy and learning: A study of a district-wide literacy initiative. *Teachers College Record, 104*(7), 1313–1344.

Stodolsky, S. (1988). *The subject matters.* Chicago: University of Chicago Press.

Stodolsky, S., & Grossman, P. L. (1995). The impact of subject matter on curricular activity: An analysis of five academic subjects. *American Research Journal, 32*(2), 227–249.

Talbert, J. E. (1995). Boundaries of teachers' professional communities in U.S. high schools: Power and precariousness of the subject department. In L. S. Siskin & J. W. Little (Eds.), *The subjects in question* (pp. 68–94). New York: Teachers College Press.

Thompson, J. D. (1967). *Organizations in action: social science bases of administrative theory.* New York: McGraw-Hill.

Timperley, H. (2005). Distributed leadership: Developing theory from practice. *Journal of Curriculum Studies, 37*(4), 395–420.

Tucker, D. J. (1981). Voluntary auspices and the behavior of social service organizations. *Social Science Review, 55,* 603–627.

Vaughan, D. (1999). The dark side of organizations: Mistake, misconduct, and disaster. *Annual Review of Sociology, 25,* 271–305.

Wehlage, G. G. (1993). *Social capital and the rebuilding of communities: Issues in restructuring schools.* Madison, WI: Center on Organization and Restructuring of Schools.

Weick, K. E. (1976). Educational organizations as loosely coupled systems." *Administrative Science Quarterly, 21,* 1–19.

Wenger, E. (1998). *Communities of practice: Learning, meaning, and identity.* Cambridge: Cambridge University Press.

Wertsch, J. (1991). *Voices of the mind: A sociocultural approach to mediated action.* Cambridge, MA: Harvard University Press.

White, R. K., & Lippitt, R. (1960). *Autocracy and democracy*. New York: Harper & Brothers.

Youngs, P., & King, M. B. (2000). *Professional development that addresses professional community in urban elementary schools*. Madison, WI: Center on Organization and Restructuring of Schools.

Yukl, G. A. (1981). *Leadership in organizations*. Englewood Cliffs, NJ: Prentice Hall.

Zollo, M., & Winter, S. (1998). *From organizational routines to dynamic capabilities* (Working paper 99-07). Philadelphia: Reginald H. Jones Center, the Wharton School, University of Pennsylvania.

About the Editors and the Contributors

Patricia Burch is an Assistant Professor in the Educational Policy Studies department at the University of Wisconsin–Madison. Her research focuses on inter-governmental processes in policy implementation and issues of equity and access.

Amy F. Coldren recently completed her doctoral dissertation titled "From Sensemaking to Knowledge Creation: A Comparison of Teacher Learning Across Two School Subjects." She is currently a postdoctoral researcher at Northwestern University where she is working with James Spillane on a book about leadership diagnosis and design.

John B. Diamond is an Assistant Professor of Education at the Harvard Graduate School of Education. He studies how race, ethnicity, and social class intersect with school leadership, policies, and practices to shape students' educational opportunities and outcomes. He has received fellowships from the National Academy of Education/Spencer Foundation and the Radcliffe Institute for Advanced Study at Harvard University. He has also received research awards from the National Science Foundation and the American Educational Research Association/Institute for Education Sciences. Diamond attended the Lansing, MI public schools and has a B.A. in sociology and political science from the University of Michigan and a Ph.D. in sociology from Northwestern University. His research has been published in *Sociology of Education, Educational Researcher, Teachers College Record, Anthropology and Educational Quarterly, Journal of Negro Education, Educational Policy, Education and Urban Society*, and *Journal of Curriculum Studies*.

Tim Hallett is an Assistant Professor in the Department of Sociology at Indiana University. He received his Ph.D. from Northwestern University in 2003. Tim's research focuses on the dynamics of social interaction in schools and other organizations. His current research examines institutional recoupling and turmoil in urban elementary schools. He has published research in *Sociology of Education* on the social construction of leadership (with James Spillane and John Diamond), in *Theory and Society* on "inhabited institutions" (with Marc Ventresca), in *Sociological Theory* on symbolic power and organizational culture, and in *The Sociological Quarterly* on how emotions "blow up" in organizations. He also is doing a project that examines the dynamics of gossip in schools (with Brent Harger and Donna Eder). Tim is an ethnographer by trade, and he has published research in *Journal of Contemporary Ethnography* on the history of ethnography (with Gary Alan Fine).

Richard R. Halverson, Assistant Professor of Educational Leadership and Policy Analysis at the University of Wisconsin–Madison, has developed research methods and theoretical frameworks to access, document, and communicate the expertise of school leaders. Halverson's research aims to bring a learning sciences perspective to the world of educational leadership. Halverson recently has applied his methods to untangling several complex areas of school leadership research, such as special education, teacher evaluation, professional community, and data-driven decisionmaking. He received his Ph.D. from Northwestern University, after 10 years experience as a school teacher and principal. His current work involves understanding how to use technologies to communicate professional practices and to build game-based environments for professional learning.

Jennifer Zoltners Sherer is a postdoctoral research associate at the Learning Research and Development Center at the University of Pittsburgh. Her research interests focus on improving K–12 school leadership practice, teaching practice, and student learning through the study and design of tools and routines. Currently, she is investigating how district policies can be designed, implemented, and evaluated using a systems perspective and system-modeling methods to aid in district reform.

James P. Spillane is the Spencer T. and Ann W. Olin Chair in Learning and Organizational Change at Northwestern University where he is a Professor of Human Development and Social Policy, Learning Sciences, and Management and Organizations. He is also a faculty fellow at the Institute for Policy Research and a senior research fellow with the Consortium for Policy Research in Education. Spillane's work explores the policy implementation process at the state, school district, school, and classroom levels, and school leadership and management. He is author of *Standards Deviation: How Local Schools Miss-Understand Policy*, *Distributed Leadership*, and numerous journal articles and book chapters.

Index